CONTINENTS IN CLOSE-UP

AUSTRALIA
AND OCEANIA

MALCOLM PORTER and KEITH LYE

RAINTREE
STECK-VAUGHN
PUBLISHERS

A Cherrytree Book
Designed and produced by
AS Publishing
Text by Keith Lye
Illustrated by Malcolm Porter and Raymond Turvey

First published 2001
by Cherrytree Press

First published in the United States 2002
by Raintree Steck-Vaughn Publishers

Library of Congress Cataloguing-in-Publication Data

Porter, Malcolm
    Australia and the Pacific / Malcolm Porter,
    Keith Lye. p. cm. – (Continents in close-up)
    Originally published: Slough, Berkshire :
    Cherrytree Press, 2001, in series; Continents
    in close-up.
    Includes bibliographical references. and index.
    ISDN 0-7398-3243-3
    1. Oceania–Juvenile literature.
    2. Australia–Juvenile literature.
    3. New Zealand–Juvenile literature.
    [1. Australia. 2. New Zealand. 3. Oceania.]
    I. Lye, Keith. II. Title. III. Continents in close-up
    (Austin, Tex.)

DU17 .P67 2001
995–dc21
                                        2001019559

ISBN 0-7398-3243-3

Printed in Hong Kong

CONTINENTS IN CLOSE-UP

AUSTRALIA
AND OCEANIA

This illustrated atlas combines maps, pictures, flags, globes,
information panels, diagrams, and charts to give an overview
of the region and a closer look at each of its countries or states.

COUNTRY CLOSE-UPS

Each double-page spread has these
features:

Introduction The author introduces the
most important facts about the country,
state or region.

Globe A globe on which you can see the
country's or state's position in the
continent and the world.

Flags Every country or state flag is shown.

Information panels Every country or state
has an information panel, which gives its
area, population, and capital, and where
appropriate its currency, religions,
languages, main towns, and government.

Pictures Important features of each
country or state are illustrated and captioned
to give a flavor of the country. You can
find out about physical features, famous
people, ordinary people, animals, plants,
places, products, and much more.

Maps Every country or state is shown on
a clear, accurate map. To get the most out
of the maps it helps to know the symbols
which are shown in the key on the
opposite page.

Land You can see by the coloring on
the map where the land is forested,
frozen, or desert.

Height Relief hill shading shows where
the mountain ranges are. Individual
mountains are marked by a triangle.

Direction All of the maps are drawn
with north at the top of the page.

Scale All of the maps are drawn to scale
so that you can find the distance
between places in miles or kilometres.

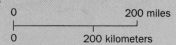

0   200 miles

0   200 kilometers

KEY TO MAPS

FIJI	Country name
Arnhem Land	Region
⌒	Country border
- - -	Country border at sea
▪	More than 1 million people*
•	More than 500,000 people
·	Less than 500,000 people
□	Country capital
★	State capital
SOUTHERN ALPS	Mountain range
▲ *Cook 4807m*	Mountain with its height

Murray	River
⬭	Lake
- - - -	Seasonal river
⬭	Seasonal lake
⬭	Island

	Forest
	Crops
	Dry grassland
	Desert
	Tundra
	Polar

*Many large cities, such as Sydney, have metropolitan populations that are greater than the city figures. Such cities have larger dot sizes to emphasize their importance.

CONTINENT CLOSE-UPS

People and Beliefs Maps of population densities; chart of percentage of population by country; chart of areas of countries; map and chart of religions.

Climate and Vegetation Map and panel on vegetation from mountain to desert; maps of winter and summer temperatures; map of annual rainfall.

Ecology and Environment Map and panel of environmental damage to land and sea; panel on vanishing islands; panel and map of natural hazards; panel of endangered species.

Economy Maps of agricultural and industrial products; chart of gross national product for individual countries; panel on per capita gross national products; map of sources of energy.

Politics and History Panel of great events; maps of exploration of Australia and the Pacific; timeline of important dates.

Index All the names on the maps and in the picture captions can be found in the index at the end of the book.

CONTENTS

Kiwi
see page 22

AUSTRALIA AND OCEANIA

Australia, New Zealand, Papua New Guinea, and the many, mostly small, islands scattered across the Pacific Ocean form a region known as Oceania. This region does not include the large island nations of eastern Asia, such as Indonesia, Japan, and the Philippines.

Although Oceania extends over a vast area, it makes up less than 6 percent of the world's land area and contains only about 0.5 percent of the world's population. Oceania is dominated by Australia, which makes up 90 percent of the region's land area. Although Australia is completely surrounded by water, it is not regarded as an island. Instead, it is considered to be the world's smallest continent.

Arafura Sea

Exploration Captain James Cook (1728-79) was a British explorer who led three expeditions to the Pacific Ocean. He was the first European to visit the east coast of Australia, which he claimed for England, and many Pacific islands, including Hawaii (which is now one of the United States).

AUSTRALIA

Cities About 85 percent of the people of Australia and New Zealand live in cities and towns. Many people work in factories or in services, such as government, business, or trade. However, both countries have important farming industries. This city is Melbourne, seen from one of its spacious suburbs.

INDIAN OCEAN

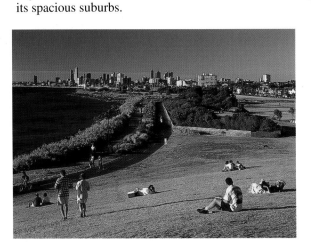

Marsupials Kangaroos are marsupials, mammals whose young are born in an immature state and reared in a pouch. With the exception of a few species, marsupials live only in Australia.

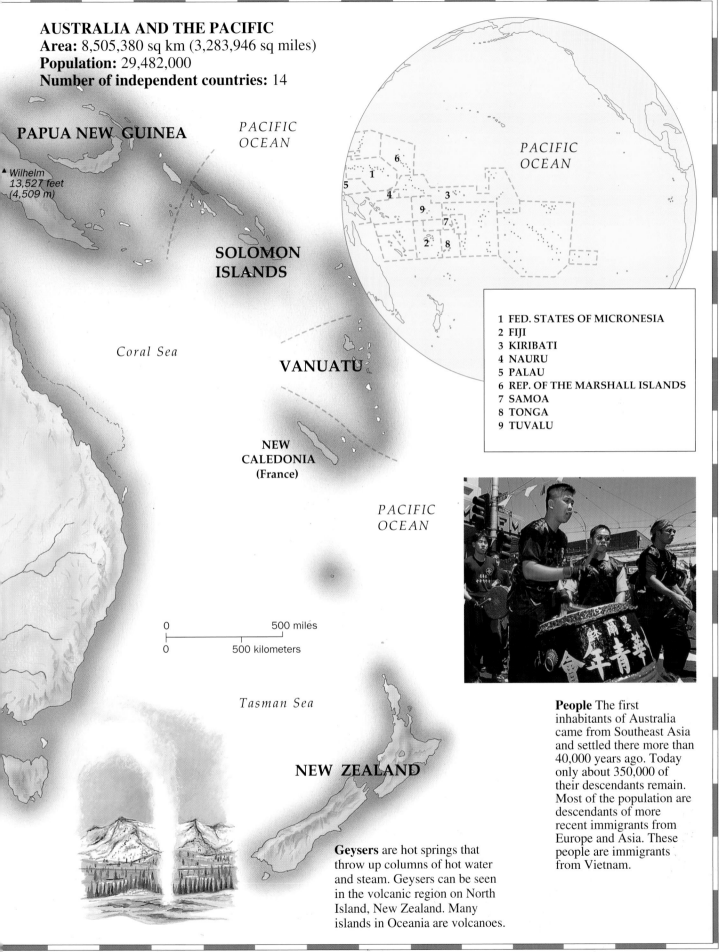

AUSTRALIA AND THE PACIFIC
Area: 8,505,380 sq km (3,283,946 sq miles)
Population: 29,482,000
Number of independent countries: 14

PAPUA NEW GUINEA

PACIFIC OCEAN

▲ *Wilhelm 13,527 feet (4,509 m)*

PACIFIC OCEAN

SOLOMON ISLANDS

Coral Sea

VANUATU

NEW CALEDONIA (France)

PACIFIC OCEAN

1 FED. STATES OF MICRONESIA
2 FIJI
3 KIRIBATI
4 NAURU
5 PALAU
6 REP. OF THE MARSHALL ISLANDS
7 SAMOA
8 TONGA
9 TUVALU

0 — 500 miles
0 — 500 kilometers

Tasman Sea

NEW ZEALAND

Geysers are hot springs that throw up columns of hot water and steam. Geysers can be seen in the volcanic region on North Island, New Zealand. Many islands in Oceania are volcanoes.

People The first inhabitants of Australia came from Southeast Asia and settled there more than 40,000 years ago. Today only about 350,000 of their descendants remain. Most of the population are descendants of more recent immigrants from Europe and Asia. These people are immigrants from Vietnam.

AUSTRALIA

Australia, which is officially called the Commonwealth of Australia, is the world's sixth-largest country. Dutch navigators explored parts of its coast in the early 17th century. European settlement began only in 1788 after the British explorer Captain James Cook had explored the east coast. He named the whole of eastern Australia New South Wales.

At first, Australia served as a British penal colony, and settlement was slow. It sped up up following gold rushes in the 1850s and 1890s. Most of these settlers came from Britain or Ireland, though since 1945 Australia has admitted settlers from Eastern Europe. Since the 1970s, other immigrants have come from Southeast Asia, Australia still retains many political ties with Britain as a member of the Britain Commonwealth.

AUSTRALIA

Area: 7,682,300 sq km (2,966,153 sq miles)
Highest point: Mt Kosciuszko in the Australian Alps (part of the Great Dividing Range) 2,228m (7,310ft)
Population: 18,532,000 (1997)
Capital: Canberra (pop 298,000)
Largest cities: Sydney (3,879,000)
Melbourne (3,283,000)
Brisbane (1,520,000)
Perth (1,295,000)
Adelaide (1,079,000)
Official language: English
Religions: Christianity (74%)
Government: Federal democracy (officially, constitutional monarchy)
Currency: Australian dollar

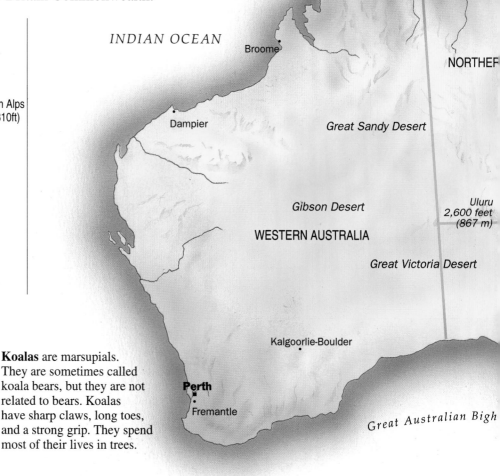

INDIAN OCEAN

Broome

NORTHER

Darwin

Dampier

Great Sandy Desert

Gibson Desert

WESTERN AUSTRALIA

Uluru
2,600 feet
(867 m)

Great Victoria Desert

Kalgoorlie-Boulder

Perth
Fremantle

Great Australian Bigh

Koalas are marsupials. They are sometimes called koala bears, but they are not related to bears. Koalas have sharp claws, long toes, and a strong grip. They spend most of their lives in trees.

Boating and other watersports are popular on Australia's coasts. But exposure to the sun is dangerous, so most Australians now make sure their skin is protected when they spend time outside.

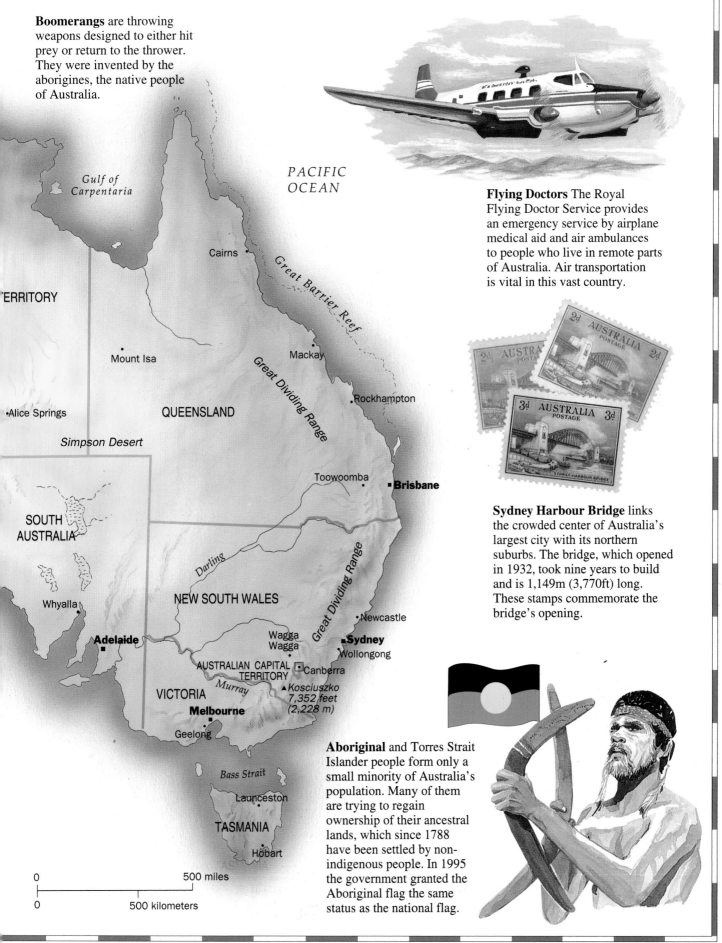

Boomerangs are throwing weapons designed to either hit prey or return to the thrower. They were invented by the aborigines, the native people of Australia.

Gulf of Carpentaria

PACIFIC OCEAN

Cairns

Great Barrier Reef

TERRITORY

Mount Isa

•Alice Springs

QUEENSLAND

Simpson Desert

Mackay

•Rockhampton

Great Dividing Range

SOUTH AUSTRALIA

Toowoomba

■**Brisbane**

Darling

NEW SOUTH WALES

Great Dividing Range

Whyalla

•Newcastle

Wagga Wagga

■**Sydney**

•Wollongong

Adelaide
■

AUSTRALIAN CAPITAL TERRITORY ⊡Canberra

Murray

▲Kosciuszko 7,352 feet (2,228 m)

VICTORIA

Melbourne
■

Geelong

Bass Strait

Launceston

TASMANIA

Hobart

0   500 miles

0   500 kilometers

Flying Doctors The Royal Flying Doctor Service provides an emergency service by airplane medical aid and air ambulances to people who live in remote parts of Australia. Air transportation is vital in this vast country.

Sydney Harbour Bridge links the crowded center of Australia's largest city with its northern suburbs. The bridge, which opened in 1932, took nine years to build and is 1,149m (3,770ft) long. These stamps commemorate the bridge's opening.

Aboriginal and Torres Strait Islander people form only a small minority of Australia's population. Many of them are trying to regain ownership of their ancestral lands, which since 1788 have been settled by non-indigenous people. In 1995 the government granted the Aboriginal flag the same status as the national flag.

WESTERN AUSTRALIA

The country of Australia consists of six states and two territories. The largest state, Western Australia, makes up nearly one-third of the country, though it has only one-tenth of its population. Much of the state is desert, but the north has hot, rainy summers and dry winters, and the southwest has dry summers and mild, rainy winters.

Minerals and resources found in Western Australia, including bauxite (aluminium ore), gold, iron ore, nickel, and oil, have helped to make Australia prosperous. Agriculture, including dairy farming, is also important in the southwest past of the state. Major crops include fruit and wheat, while sheep are raised in dry areas.

WESTERN AUSTRALIA

Area: 2,525,000 sq km (974,908 sq miles)
Highest point: Mount Meharry 1,251m (4,104 ft)
Population: 1,726,000 (1996)
Capital and largest city: Perth (pop 1,295,000)
Other large urban areas: Mandurah (42,000)
Kalgoorlie-Boulder (30,000)
Bunbury (28,000)
Floral emblem: Red and green kangaroo paw
Animal emblem: Numbat
Bird emblem: Black swan

Pearls and mother-of-pearl, the lining of the oyster shells in which pearls form, were obtained from Shark Bay, Western Australia, as early as 1850. In recent years, Australian and Japanese companies have set up pearl farms in both Western Australia and Queensland.

Gold and Diamonds Most of Australia's gold comes from Western Australia. Rich diamond fields were also discovered in the state in the 1970s. By the 1990s Australia led the world in diamond production.

Pinnacles Desert, on the coast north of Perth, consists of a forest of thin peaks made of limestone. This area is part of the Nambung National Park. Australia has set up many national parks to protect its natural wonders and wildlife.

Indian Ocean

The Indian Ocean extends from India in the north to Antarctica in the south. It washes the shores of western and southern Australia as far as the west coast of Tasmania. The east coast of Tasmania faces the Pacific Ocean.

Area: about 74,000,000 sq km
(29,000,000 sq miles)
Average depth: 3,840 m (about 12,600 ft)
Deepest point: 7,725 m (25,344 ft)

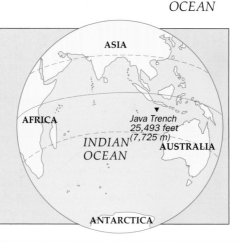

INDIAN OCEAN

Dampier
Port Hedland
Karratha
Marble Bar
Onslow
Hamersley Range
Ashburton
Meharry
4,128 feet
(1,251 m)
Gascoyne
Carnarvon
Shark Bay
Murchison
Geraldton
INDIAN OCEAN

Northam
Perth ★
Fremantle
Mandurah
Bunbury
Katanning
Swan
Manjimup
Albany

ASIA
AFRICA
Java Trench
25,493 feet
(7,725 m)
INDIAN OCEAN
AUSTRALIA
ANTARCTICA

Numbat The numbat is the animal emblem of Western Australia. It is a marsupial, but the females do not have a pouch. The babies simply cling to their mother's teats and fur. Adult numbats live on termites, eating many thousands every day. The species is endangered and protected by law.

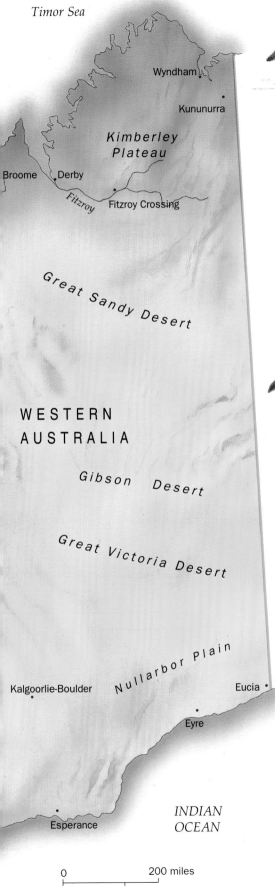

Timor Sea

Wyndham

Kununurra

Kimberley Plateau

Broome • Derby

Fitzroy • Fitzroy Crossing

Great Sandy Desert

WESTERN AUSTRALIA

Gibson Desert

Great Victoria Desert

Nullarbor Plain

Kalgoorlie-Boulder

Eucia •

Eyre •

Esperance •

INDIAN OCEAN

0 — 200 miles

0 — 200 kilometers

Wave Rock is a famous scenic wonder that lies about 390 km (242 miles) east of Perth. It is made of granite, a hard rock, but its wrinkled face has been worn away by natural forces.

Kangaroo paw is the floral emblem of Western Australia. The heads of the flowers are covered by dense wool that resembles a kangaroo's paw. There are about 10 varieties of kangaroo paw.

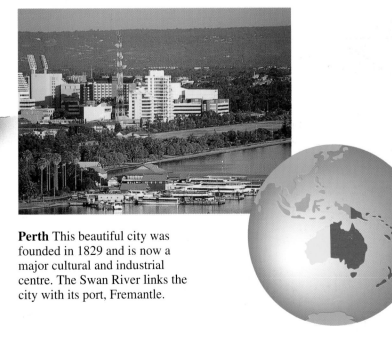

Perth This beautiful city was founded in 1829 and is now a major cultural and industrial centre. The Swan River links the city with its port, Fremantle.

NORTHERN TERRITORY

By far the largest of Australia's two territories is Northern Territory. The region has been essentially self-governing since 1978. Nearly one-quarter of its people are Aborigines and the territory contains many sacred Aboriginal sites, including the famous Uluru (or Ayers Rock).

Northern Territory covers nearly one-sixth of Australia, but it is the most sparsely populated part of the country. The tropical north has a hot, rainy climate, but the south is mainly desert. Northern Territory is known for its fine scenery and its mineral deposits, which are its greatest source of wealth. Its minerals and resources include bauxite, manganese, oil, natural gas, and uranium.

NORTHERN TERRITORY

Area: 1,346,200 sq km (519,771 sq miles)
Highest point: Mount Zeil 1,510 m (4,854 ft)
Population: 299,000 (1996)
Capital and largest city: Darwin (pop 82,000)
Other large urban areas: Alice Springs (20,000)
Floral emblem: Sturt's desert rose
Animal emblem: Red kangaroo
Bird emblem: Wedge-tailed eagle

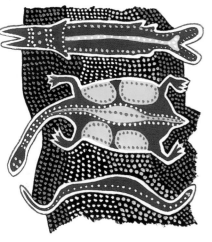

Matthew Flinders (1774-1814), a British navigator, sailed around Australia between 1801 and 1803. He mapped much of the coastline and proved that there was no strait (natural waterway) that cut through Australia.

Aboriginal art In ancient times, aboriginal artists painted on cave walls and on bark. Many paintings had religious significance, while others depicted traditional ways of life. Today, aboriginal art is sold for large sums of money.

Sturt's desert rose, the floral emblem of Northern Territory, is named after the explorer Charles Sturt. Its seven petals, which are shown on the territory's flag, symbolize the six states of Australia and Northern Territory.

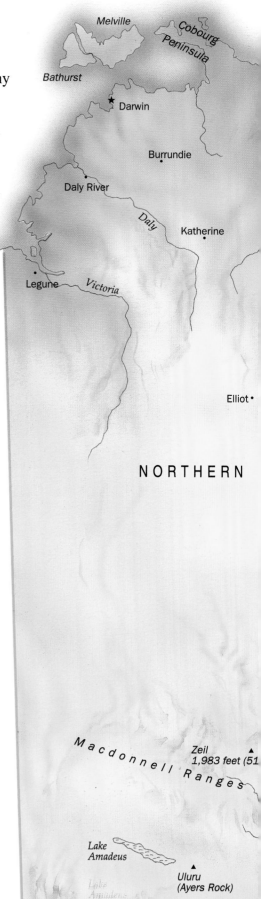

Melville

Cobourg Peninsula

Bathurst

★ Darwin

Burrundie

Daly River

Daly

Katherine

Legune

Victoria

Elliot

NORTHERN

Macdonnell Ranges

Zeil
1,983 feet (51

Lake
Amadeus

Lake
Amadeus

Uluru
(Ayers Rock)

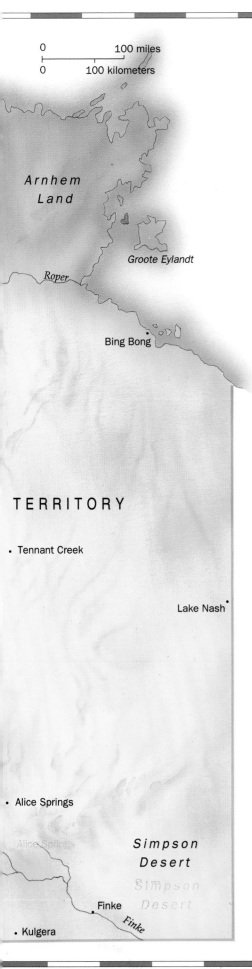

Arnhem
Land

Groote Eylandt

Roper

Bing Bong

TERRITORY

• Tennant Creek

Lake Nash

• Alice Springs

Alice Springs

Simpson
Desert

Simpson
Desert

Finke

Finke

• Kulgera

Darwin, capital of Northern Territory, is small, but it is a major communications center. The harbor on which it stands was named after the naturalist Charles Darwin in 1839. The first settlement on the harbor was not built until 1869.

Crocodiles Two types of crocodile live in the tropical regions of northern Australia. Saltwater crocodiles live in river mouths where tides bring in salt water. Freshwater crocodiles live in inland streams and lakes. Both species are protected, though they are probably no longer endangered.

Uluru is an aboriginal word meaning ''great pebble.'' It is the aboriginal name for a huge, red rock outcrop, formerly known as Ayers Rock, in the southern part of Northern Territory. Uluru is a major tourist attraction.

Kakadu National Park, which lies east of Darwin, is a World Heritage Site. About one-third of Australia's bird species can be seen there, especially waterbirds. The park also contains the world's largest and best-preserved body of rock art.

SOUTH AUSTRALIA

South Australia is the third-largest Australian state. About four-fifths of the land is desert, covered by sand, or gibber, the local name for stony desert. The map of South Australia shows several lakes, including lakes Eyre and Gairdner. But these lakes only contain water after infrequent storms. Most of the time, they are dry, their beds covered by salt.

Most South Australians live in the southeast part of the state, which has hot, dry summers and mild, moist winters. This is a region of rich farmland, where barley, grapes, and wheat are grown. Sheep and cattle are also raised on the region's lush pasture land.

SOUTH AUSTRALIA

Area: 984,000 sq km (379,925 sq miles)
Highest point: Mount Woodroffe 1,440 m (4,724 ft)
Population: 1,428,000 (1996)
Capital and largest city: Adelaide (pop 1,079,000)
Other large urban areas: Whyalla (23,600)
Mount Gambier (22,000)
Port Augusta (14,000)
Floral emblem: Sturt's desert pea
Animal emblem: Hairy-nosed wombat
Bird emblem: Piping shrike

Opals Australia is the world's leading producer of opal, a beautiful gemstone. The country's chief center of opal production is Coober Pedy, South Australia. It lies about 700 km (435 miles) northwest of Adelaide.

Sturt's desert pea, the floral emblem of South Australia, is named after the explorer Charles Sturt. Large numbers of these plants, with their deep red flowers, bloom over vast areas after rainfall. The plants produce hard, narrow brown pods, each containing many seeds that lie dormant until the next downpour.

Road trains are used to transport goods over huge distances in Australia. One high-powered truck pulls three or four large trailers along routes such as the Stuart Highway from Adelaide to Perth, which is 3,100 km (1,926 miles) long.

Woodroffe
▲ 4,752 feet (1,440 m)
M u s g r a v e   R a n g e
Welbourn Hill

G r e a t   V i c t o r i a   D e s e r t

Maralinga
Cook
S O U T H
N u l l a r b o r   P l a i n
Tarcoola
Yalatta
Coorabie
Ceduna

G r e a t   A u s t r a l i a n   B i g h t

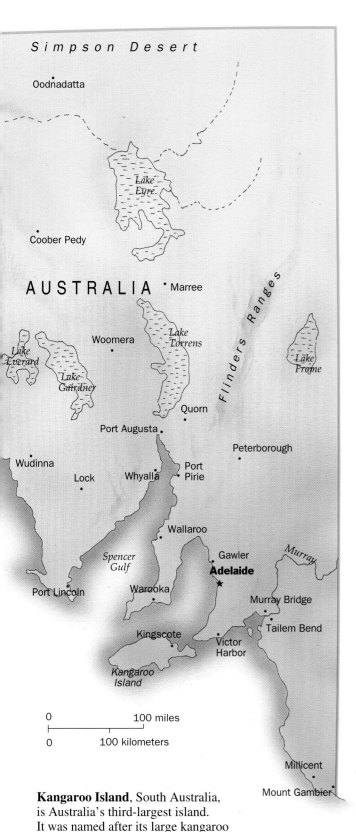

Simpson Desert

- Oodnadatta
- Coober Pedy

AUSTRALIA
- Marree

Lake Eyre

Flinders Ranges

- Woomera
- Lake Everard
- Lake Gairdner
- Lake Torrens
- Lake Frome
- Quorn
- Port Augusta
- Peterborough
- Wudinna
- Lock
- Whyalla
- Port Pirie
- Wallaroo
- Spencer Gulf
- Gawler
- Murray
- **Adelaide** ★
- Port Lincoln
- Warooka
- Murray Bridge
- Tailem Bend
- Kingscote
- Victor Harbor
- Kangaroo Island
- Millicent
- Mount Gambier

```
0               100 miles
|---------------|
0               100 kilometers
```

Salt pans are huge dried-up "lakes" with a surface of salt. Because they are flat, they have often been used for car speed trials.

Wheat is grown principally in a broad arc from southeastern South Australia, through Victoria and New South Wales, into southeastern Queensland. Another wheat-growing area is in Western Australia.

Adelaide, South Australia's capital, is a major port, with a wide range of industries. The first colonists arrived in 1836. This carefully planned city is known for its many churches and the scenic coastlands and hills that surround it.

Kangaroo Island, South Australia, is Australia's third-largest island. It was named after its large kangaroo population. The island has a sanctuary for the Australian fur seal on the south coast of Sea Bay. Its other attractions include fairy penguins and its scenic coastline.

QUEENSLAND

Queensland, the second-largest state of Australia, has a warm climate and is often called the "Sunshine State." Off its coast lies the Great Barrier Reef, the world's largest coral formation. The Great Barrier Reef and the state's coastal resorts attract many tourists. The chief resort area is the Gold Coast, south of Brisbane. This area extends along the coast into New South Wales.

Queensland is a major producer of sugar cane, while beef, dairy cattle, and sheep are also important. Queensland has coal, copper, and lead deposits, and manufacturing is a leading activity, especially in Brisbane.

QUEENSLAND

Area: 1,727,000 sq km (666,798 sq miles)
Highest point: Mount Bartle Frere 1,611 m (5,285 ft)
Population: 3,369,000 (1996)
Capital and largest city: Brisbane (pop 1,520,000)
Other large urban areas: Gold Coast-Tweed, including part in New South Wales, (368,000)
Townsville (123,000)
Sunshine Coast (162,000)
Cairns (109,000)
Floral emblem: Cooktown orchid
Animal emblem: Koala
Bird emblem: Brolga

Pineapples are grown in Queensland. Bananas also thrive in the tropical conditions. In cooler areas, temperate fruits, such as apples, are grown. The most valuable crops are grains, including barley, maize, sorghum, and wheat.

Mount Isa in western Queensland has some of the world's richest mines. Deposits of copper, lead, silver, and zinc, which are found close together, are all mined at Mount Isa. Queensland is also a leading coal producer.

Cattle ranching is Queensland's most valuable farming activity. The main ranching area is in east-central Queensland. Dairy farming is important in the southeast, especially around Brisbane.

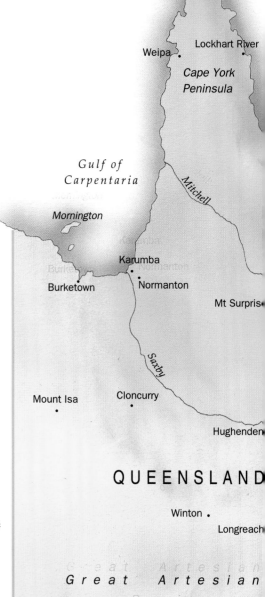

Cape York
Bamaga
Weipa
Lockhart River
Cape York Peninsula
Gulf of Carpentaria
Mitchell
Mornington
Karumba
Normanton
Burketown
Mt Surprise
Saxby
Mount Isa
Cloncurry
Hughenden
QUEENSLAND
Winton
Longreach
Great Artesian Basin
Birdsville

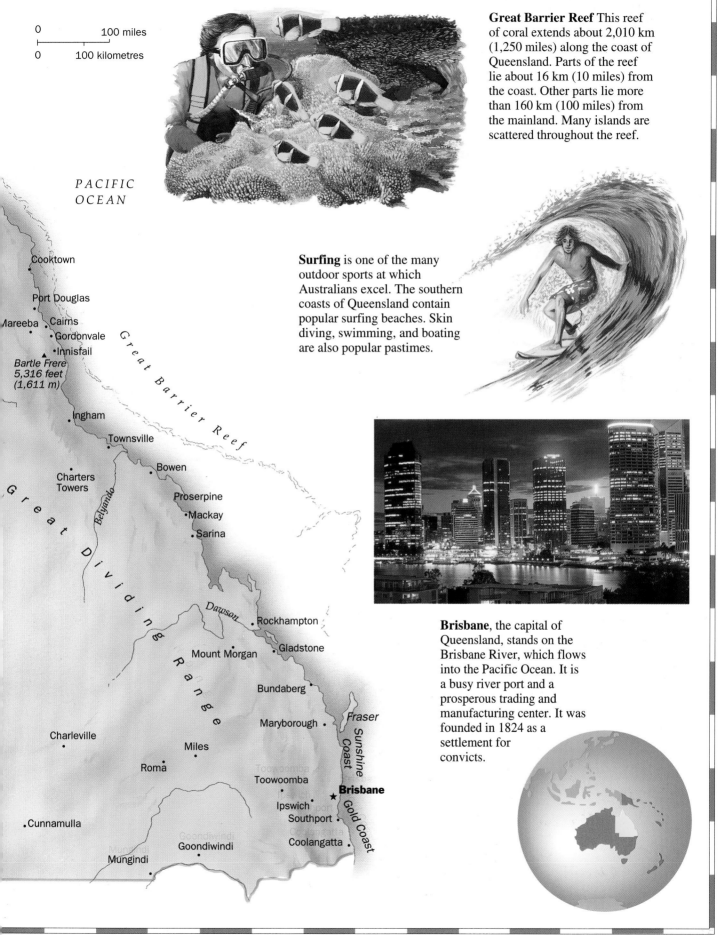

| 0 | 100 miles |
| 0 | 100 kilometres |

Great Barrier Reef This reef of coral extends about 2,010 km (1,250 miles) along the coast of Queensland. Parts of the reef lie about 16 km (10 miles) from the coast. Other parts lie more than 160 km (100 miles) from the mainland. Many islands are scattered throughout the reef.

Surfing is one of the many outdoor sports at which Australians excel. The southern coasts of Queensland contain popular surfing beaches. Skin diving, swimming, and boating are also popular pastimes.

Brisbane, the capital of Queensland, stands on the Brisbane River, which flows into the Pacific Ocean. It is a busy river port and a prosperous trading and manufacturing center. It was founded in 1824 as a settlement for convicts.

PACIFIC OCEAN

Cooktown

Port Douglas

Mareeba · Cairns
· Gordonvale
· Innisfail
▲ Bartle Frere
5,316 feet
(1,611 m)

Great Barrier Reef

· Ingham

Townsville

Bowen

Charters Towers

Belyando

Proserpine
· Mackay
· Sarina

Great Dividing Range

Dawson

Rockhampton

Mount Morgan · Gladstone

Bundaberg

Charleville

Miles

Maryborough · Fraser

Roma

Toowoomba

Sunshine Coast

Ipswich ★ **Brisbane**

Southport

Cunnamulla

Goondiwindi

Coolangatta

Gold Coast

Mungindi

15

NEW SOUTH WALES

New South Wales is the richest and most developed Australian state. Although it ranks fourth in area, it contains more people than any other state. The cities of Sydney, Newcastle, and Wollongong contain about three-quarters of the state's people. New South Wales was originally the name for a British colony that covered the whole of eastern Australia. It assumed roughly its present borders in 1863.

Enclosed in the southeastern corner of New South Wales is the small Australian Capital Territory. This area was chosen as the site of Australia's federal capital, Canberra, in 1909.

NEW SOUTH WALES

Area: 801,600 sq km (309,500 sq miles)
Highest point: Mount Kosciuszko 2,228 m (7,310 ft)
Population: 6,039,000 (1996)
Capital and largest city: Sydney (pop 3,879,000)
Other large urban areas: Newcastle (464,000)
Wollongong (256,000)
Floral emblem: Waratah
Animal emblem: Platypus
Bird emblem: Kookaburra

AUSTRALIAN CAPITAL TERRITORY

Area: 2,400 sq km (927 sq miles)
Population: 299,000 (1996)

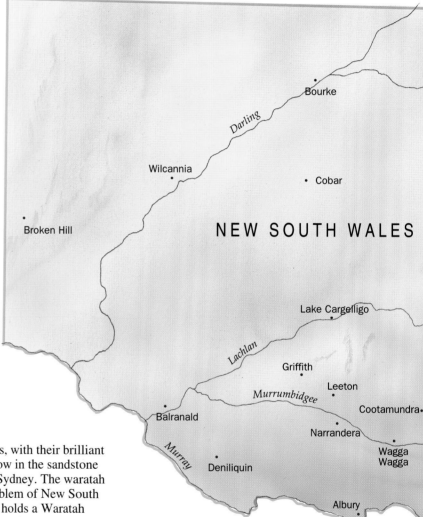

Waratah plants, with their brilliant red flowers, grow in the sandstone region around Sydney. The waratah is the floral emblem of New South Wales. Sydney holds a Waratah Spring Festival each October.

Canberra, in Australian Capital Territory, is the national capital, where the parliament, consisting of the Senate and House of Representatives, meets. The layout of this handsome city was originally planned by an American architect, Walter Burley Griffin.

Washing machines are among many products made in New South Wales, which is Australia's top manufacturing state. Others include cars, chemicals, clothing, farm implements, fertilizers, glassware, iron and steel, machinery, paper, and textiles.

Blue Mountains These scenic mountains west of Sydney are part of the Great Dividing Range. Once they formed a daunting barrier to settlers and kept them from reaching the interior plains, but a road was built through the mountains in 1815.

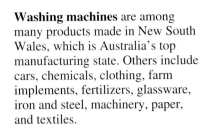

Platypus The platypus is often called a duckbill, because it has a bill like a duck's. It is one of only two kinds of mammals that lay eggs, the other being the echidna. Both live only in Australia.

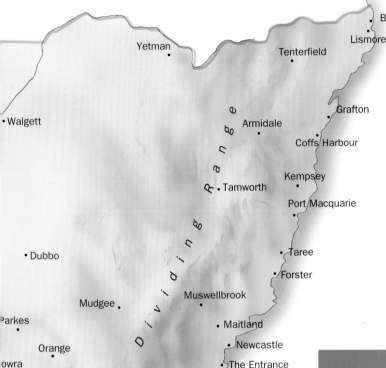

Byron Bay
Lismore
Yetman
Tenterfield
Grafton
Walgett
Armidale
Coffs Harbour
Great Dividing Range
Kempsey
Tamworth
Port Macquarie
Dubbo
Taree
Forster
Parkes
Mudgee
Muswellbrook
Orange
Maitland
owra
Newcastle
Young
The Entrance
Gosford
Sydney
Yass
Campbelltown
Goulburn
Wollongong
Kiama
Nowra
Canberra
AUSTRALIAN
CAPITAL
TERRITORY
Cooma
Eden

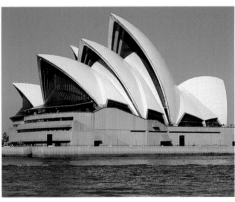

Sydney Opera House stands on a peninsula that juts into Sydney Harbour. Its sail-like roofs, made of overlapping shells, give it an unforgettable appearance. It opened in 1973.

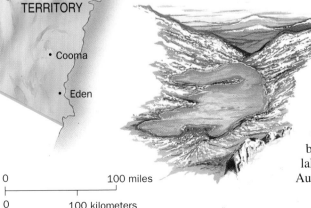

Kosciuszko National Park, in southeastern New South Wales, is a major tourist and ski resort. It lies in the Australian Alps, part of the Great Dividing Range. Among its beautiful snowy mountains and lakes is Mount Kosciuszko, Australia's highest peak.

0   100 miles

0   100 kilometers

VICTORIA

Victoria is the smallest of Australia's mainland states. Yet, with about 20 people to every square kilometer (50 per square mile), it is the most densely populated part of the country. Victoria has a higher proportion of people from non-English-speaking countries than any other state. It contains sizeable communities of Italian, Greek, and Vietnamese people.

Victoria has large areas of fertile land. Farming is important, but today the state's prosperity comes mainly from industry. Victoria produces brown coal, oil, and natural gas, together with a wide range of manufactured products.

VICTORIA

Area: 227,600 sq km (87,877 sq miles)
Highest point: Mount Bogong 1,986 m (6,526 ft)
Population: 4,374,000 (1996)
Capital and largest city: Melbourne (pop 3,283,000)
Other large urban areas: Geelong (125,000)
Ballarat (65,000)
Bendigo (60,000)
Floral emblem: Pink heath
Animal emblem: Leadbeater's possum
Bird emblem: Helmeted honeyeater

Australian Rules football is a fast, exciting form of football, invented by Australians and played only in Australia and Papua New Guinea. Other popular team sports include cricket, rugby, and soccer.

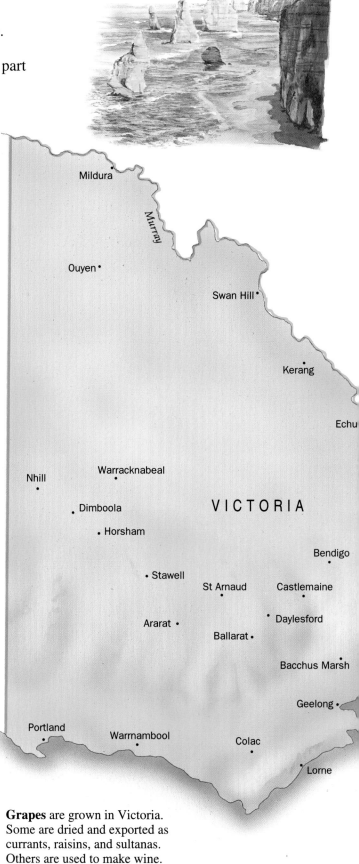

Grapes are grown in Victoria. Some are dried and exported as currants, raisins, and sultanas. Others are used to make wine. Top-quality Australian wines are now sold around the world.

Twelve Apostles is the name of a series of limestone stacks along the southwest coast of Victoria. Stacks are fragments of the coast that have been cut off from the shore by the continuous battering of sea waves.

Sheep More than two-fifths of Victoria's farmland is used to raise sheep. Victoria is a major exporter of lamb, sheep, and wool. Beef and dairy products are also important. Major crops include wheat and other grains, hay, and potatoes.

Murray River This river rises in the Snowy Mountains and is Australia's longest permanently flowing river. It is used to produce hydroelectricity and to irrigate the land. Tourists take pleasure trips on its paddle steamers.

Ned Kelly (1855-80) was the best known of Australia's bushrangers, or outlaws. He was born in Victoria. He and members of his gang wore armor to protect their bodies from gunfire. Many poor people regarded him as a hero.

Melbourne is Australia's second-largest city, after Sydney. It contains about three-quarters of Victoria's population. It was founded on the Yarra River at the head of Port Phillip Bay in 1835. It is now a major commercial, financial and industrial center.

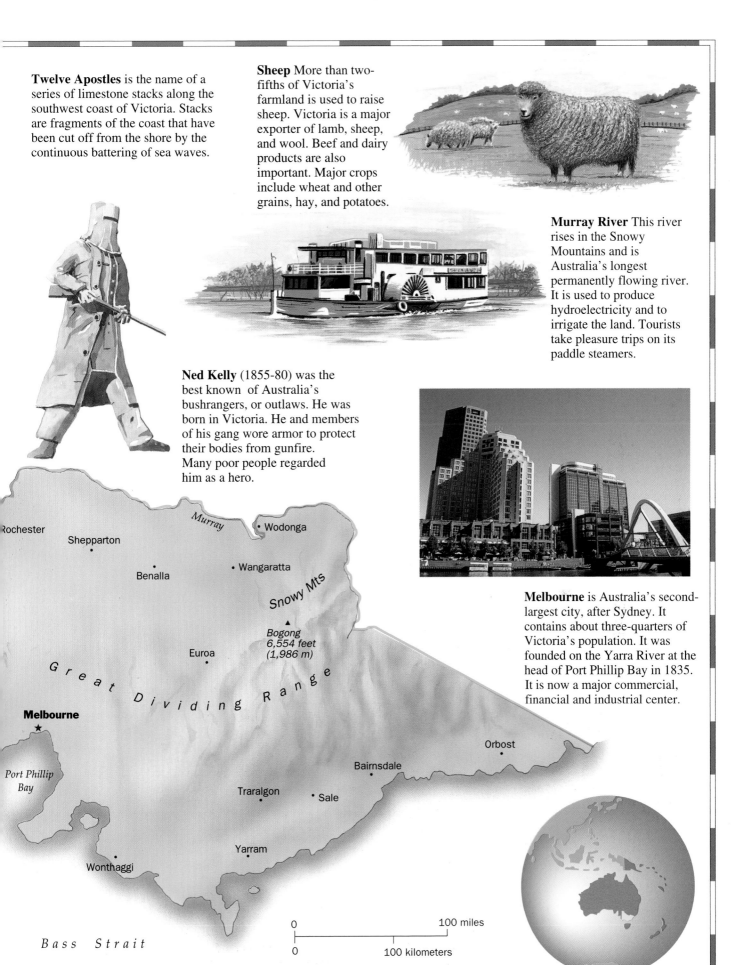

Rochester

Shepparton

Murray

Wodonga

Benalla

Wangaratta

Snowy Mts

Euroa

▲ Bogong
6,554 feet
(1,986 m)

Great Dividing Range

Melbourne ★

Port Phillip Bay

Orbost

Bairnsdale

Traralgon • Sale

Yarram

Wonthaggi

Bass Strait

0   100 miles

0   100 kilometers

TASMANIA

Tasmania, Australia's smallest state, is separated from mainland Australia by the 240-km (149-mile) wide Bass Strait. The island was discovered by the Dutch navigator Abel Tasman in 1642. He named it Van Diemen's Land, after the governor of the Dutch East Indies, but the British renamed it Tasmania in 1855.

Tasmania is mountainous, with a rainy, temperate climate. Its resources include valuable minerals, forests, and rivers that are used to produce hydroelectricity. Farmers raise cattle and sheep and grow crops such as apples and potatoes.

King

• Grassy

Montagu • Stanley
Burnie •
Ulverstone •

Lake Mackintosh

Corinna •

Ossa
5,336 feet
(1,617 m)
• Queenstown

INDIAN OCEAN

Lake Pedder

TASMANIA

Area: 67,800 sq km (26,178 sq miles)
Highest point: Mount Ossa 1,617 m (5,305 ft)
Population: 460,000 (1996)
Capital: Hobart (pop 196,000)
Other large urban areas: Launceston (96,000)
Devonport (24,000)
Burnie (19,000)
Floral emblem: Tasmanian blue gum
Animal emblem (unofficial): Tasmanian devil
Bird emblem (unofficial): Green rosella parrot

Hydroelectric dams have been built on many of Tasmania's rivers to take advantage of the heavy rainfall and run-off from the mountains. The electricity powers industries that manufacture refined metals, including zinc, iron ore, copper, and tin, wood and paper products, and processed farm products.

Abel Tasman (1603-59), a Dutch navigator, sailed all the way round Australia in 1642 but never sighted the mainland. He did visit Tasmania, which is named after him. On a second voyage in 1644, he explored parts of the northern and western coasts of Australia.

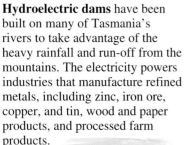

Tasmanian blue gum
This beautiful eucalyptus tree is the state's floral emblem. Forests cover nearly half of Tasmania, with beech and myrtle being common in the wettest areas and eucalyptus in areas with rainfall of 76-150 cm (30-59 in).

Apples Tasmania was once called the "Apple Isle," but apples ceased to be a major crop after the state lost its British markets in the 1970s, when Britain became part of the European Economic Community (now the European Union, or EU). British membership of the EU has weakened ties between Australia and Britain.

Bass Strait

Tasmanian Devil This fierce marsupial, which measures up to 39 inches (1 meter) long, feeds on animals, living or dead. Today it lives only on Tasmania, though once it lived on the Australian mainland. The Tasmanian wolf, another marsupial native to the island, is now thought to be extinct.

Hobart, the capital of Tasmania, is an important port on the estuary of the Derwent River. The city was founded in 1804 as a port and whaling center. Industries in the city now produce cement, wood pulp, and metal products.

Palana

Flinders

Cape Barren

George Town

Gladstone

Tasman Sea

Devonport

Launceston

St Marys

Great Lake

Ross

Bronte

Swansea

Coles Bay

TASMANIA

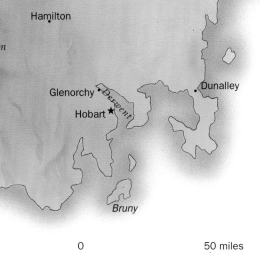

Hamilton

Lake Gordon

Dunalley

Glenorchy

Hobart

Hobart Cup The Sydney-Hobart yacht race covers 1,134 km (630 nautical miles). It starts on December 26 each year. The fastest yachts cover the distance in little over three days. The first race was held in 1945.

Bruny

```
0                    50 miles
├────┬────┬────┬────┤
0              50 kilometers
```

NEW ZEALAND

New Zealand is a remote country that lies about 1,600 km (994 miles) southeast of Australia. Its first human inhabitants were the Maori, who came to Aotearoa, their name for New Zealand, from islands to the northeast more than 1,200 years ago. The first European to reach the islands was the Dutch navigator Abel Tasman in 1642.

The Dutch did not settle, however, and in 1769, Captain James Cook rediscovered New Zealand and charted the coasts of the main islands. The first British settlers arrived in 1814. Today most New Zealanders are descendants of British settlers. The Maori number about 520,000. Another 560,000 people have Maori ancestors.

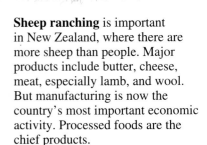

Sheep ranching is important in New Zealand, where there are more sheep than people. Major products include butter, cheese, meat, especially lamb, and wool. But manufacturing is now the country's most important economic activity. Processed foods are the chief products.

 NEW ZEALAND

Area: 270,534 sq km (104,454 sq miles)
Highest point: Mount Cook (Aorangi in Maori), in the Southern Alps, 3,764 m (12,349 ft)
Population: 3,761,000
Capital: Wellington (pop 335,000)
Largest cities: Auckland (998,000)
Dunedin (331,000)
Hamilton (159,000)
Hastings and Napier (114,000)
Palmerston North (74,000)
Official language: English
Religions: Christianity (61%)
Government: Parliamentary democracy (officially, constitutional monarchy)
Currency: New Zealand dollar

Kiwi fruit are grown in New Zealand, especially in the area around the Bay of Plenty on North Island. Kiwi fruit, which were called Chinese gooseberries until the New Zealanders renamed them, are exported to many countries.

Tasman Sea

Kiwis are flightless birds that live only in New Zealand. They are seldom seen because they come out only at night. They live in forests and forage for worms and insects on the ground.

War chants The Maori are famous for their haka, or war chants. These are shouted in a rhythmic way by Maori warriors – and rugby teams. One well-known chant, *Ka-mate, ka-mate*, is supposed to have been composed by a famous chief named Te Rauparaha.

South Island

Mount Cook (Aorangi)
12,421 feet ▲
(3,764 m)

Southern Alps

Timaru

Dunedin

Invercargill

Stewart Island

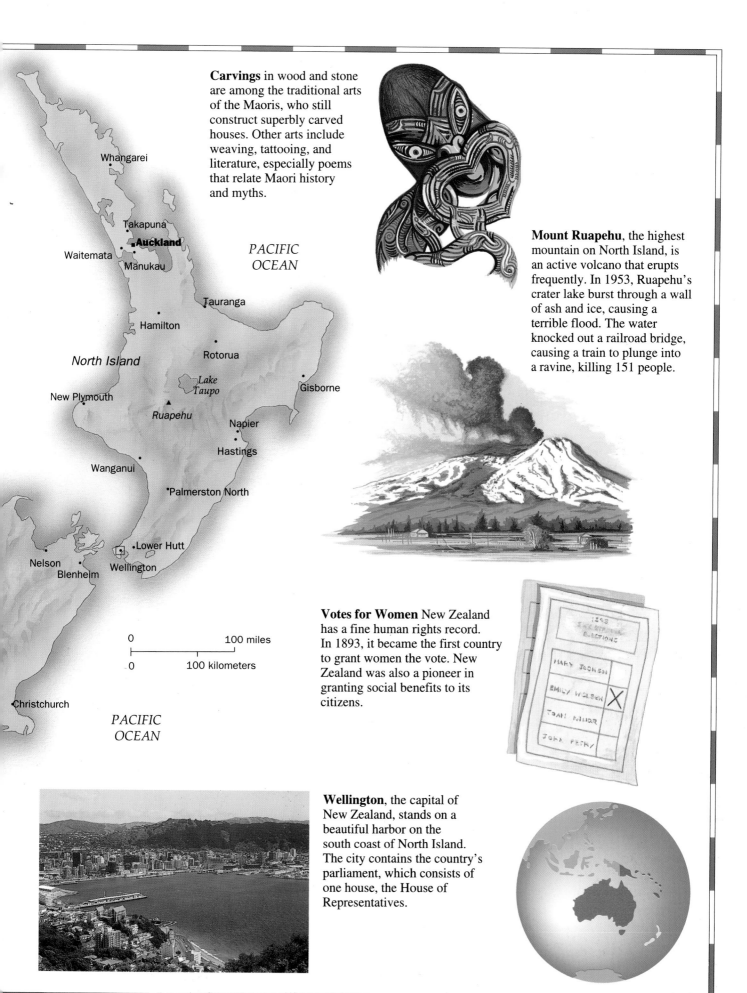

Carvings in wood and stone are among the traditional arts of the Maoris, who still construct superbly carved houses. Other arts include weaving, tattooing, and literature, especially poems that relate Maori history and myths.

Whangarei

Takapuna
Auckland
Waitemata
Manukau

PACIFIC OCEAN

Tauranga

Hamilton

North Island

Rotorua

New Plymouth

Lake Taupo

Gisborne

▲ *Ruapehu*

Napier

Hastings

Wanganui

Palmerston North

Lower Hutt

Nelson
Blenheim
Wellington

0   100 miles

0   100 kilometers

Christchurch

PACIFIC OCEAN

Mount Ruapehu, the highest mountain on North Island, is an active volcano that erupts frequently. In 1953, Ruapehu's crater lake burst through a wall of ash and ice, causing a terrible flood. The water knocked out a railroad bridge, causing a train to plunge into a ravine, killing 151 people.

Votes for Women New Zealand has a fine human rights record. In 1893, it became the first country to grant women the vote. New Zealand was also a pioneer in granting social benefits to its citizens.

Wellington, the capital of New Zealand, stands on a beautiful harbor on the south coast of North Island. The city contains the country's parliament, which consists of one house, the House of Representatives.

NORTH ISLAND

North Island is the smallest of New Zealand's two largest islands. It contains hilly regions in the south, a central volcanic region, and, in the north, peninsulas that jut into the Pacific Ocean. The volcanic region contains three active volcanoes: Mount Ruapehu, the highest, Mount Ngauruhoe, and Mount Tongariro. There are also many hot springs and geysers. Much of North Island was formed by volcanic activity within the last four million years.

North Island contains Wellington, the country's capital, and Auckland, the largest city and chief manufacturing center.

0   50 miles

0   50 kilometers

Tasman Sea

Auckland is the largest city in New Zealand. It has grown rapidly as more and more people have been attracted by its semi-tropical climate and casual lifestyle. Most work in the city center and live in sprawling suburbs connected by roads and highways.

Dairy farming is a major activity on North Island, where most of the country's 8 million cattle are raised. Butter and cheese are the leading dairy products on the island and are among New Zealand's leading exports. Dried milk is also exported. The northern part of North Island has a warm climate, and subtropical crops, such as avocados and citrus fruits, are grown there.

Mount Egmont is a dormant (sleeping) volcano that last erupted more than 300 years ago. A Maori legend tells how a lover's quarrel between Egmont (Taranaki in Maori) and Mount Tongariro explains its isolated position in the southwestern part of North Island.

North Cape

Whangarei

Dargaville

Hauraki Gulf

East Coast Bays

Takapuna

Auckland
Mount Roskill   Papatoete
Waitemata
Manukau
Papakura

Hamilton

New Plymouth

▲
Egmont
8,309 feet
(2,518 m)

Wangan...

Wanganui

Palmerston Nort...

Upper Hutt
Porirua
Lower Hut...
Wellington

Cook Strait

PACIFIC
OCEAN

Sailing is a popular leisure activity. The country's first regatta was held in Wellington in 1841. The Auckland Regatta, one of the world's largest one-day sailing events, was first held in 1850.

Rugby is perhaps the most popular team sport in New Zealand, which is home to many clubs and teams. The national team is called the All Blacks because of the color of its jerseys, shorts, and socks.

Great
Barrier I

Coromandel
Peninsula

• Waihi

Bay of Plenty

• Tauranga

Lake Rotorua

Rotorua

Whakatane

Waikato

Lake Taupo

Lake Waikaremoana

Gisborne

▲ Ngauruhoe 2291 m
Ruapehu 2796 m

Wairoa

Mahia Peninsula

• Napier

Hastings

PACIFIC
OCEAN

Masterton

Kauri trees are among the biggest trees in the world, some reaching heights of 45 m (148 ft) with trunks 20 m (66 ft) in circumference. In the past so many were cut down for their timber or burned in bush fires that they were in danger of extinction. Now most of them are protected in state forests.

Steam rising from the ground in volcanic areas is used by power stations to generate electricity. Hydroelectric power is also important in New Zealand. On North Island, the Waikato River has several hydroelectric plants.

SOUTH ISLAND

The Southern Alps on South Island contain the country's highest peak, Mount Cook, or Aorangi, its Maori name, which means "cloud piercer." Huge sheets of ice, called glaciers, fill high mountain valleys. Long ago, the glaciers flowed down to sea level, carving out deep valleys, which are now sea inlets called fjords.

On the east-central coast of South Island lie the Canterbury Plains, a major grain-growing region. Livestock farming is important in the southeast. The country's third-largest island, Stewart Island, lies off the south coast of South Island.

Grapes grow well on South Island, and many vineyards produce wine for export. Other important crops include apples, barley, pears, potatoes, and wheat.

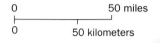

0   50 miles

0   50 kilometers

Southern Alps This young mountain range, which forms the backbone of South Island, was pushed up from the ocean floor in the last 10 to 15 million years. Evergreen forests cover its slopes. At higher elevations there are glaciers and ice fields.

Milford Sound is one of many fjords in the southwest coastal area of Fjordland. It is the only fjord that can be reached by road. The whole coast is marked by steep-sided inlets with hundreds of waterfalls and magnificent scenery.

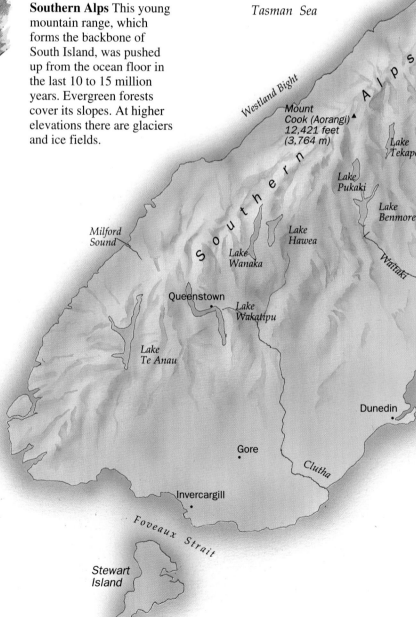

Tasman Sea

Westland Bight

Southern Alps

Mount Cook (Aorangi) ▲ 12,421 feet (3,764 m)

Lake Tekapo

Lake Pukaki

Lake Benmore

Waitaki

Milford Sound

Lake Hawea

Lake Wanaka

Queenstown

Lake Wakatipu

Lake Te Anau

Dunedin

Gore

Clutha

Invercargill

Foveaux Strait

Stewart Island

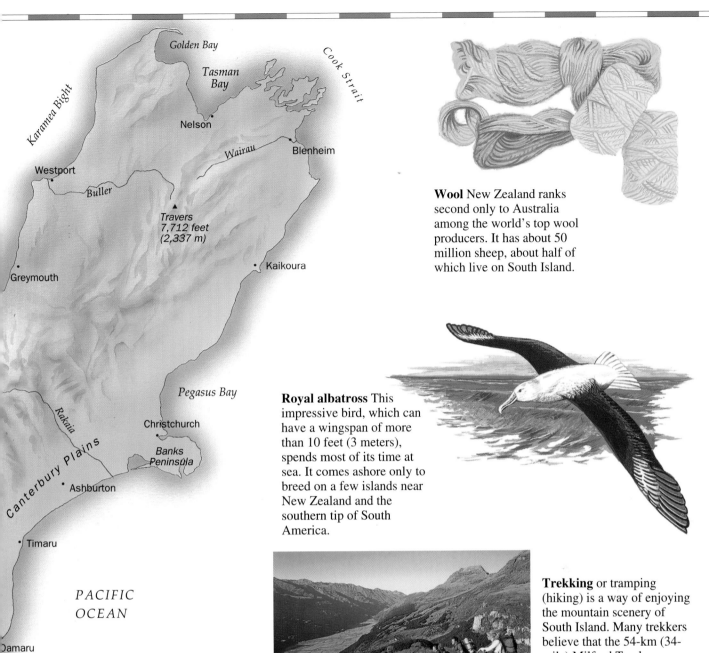

Golden Bay

Tasman Bay

Cook Strait

Karamea Bight

Nelson

Wairau

Blenheim

Westport

Buller

Travers
7,712 feet
(2,337 m)

Greymouth

Kaikoura

Pegasus Bay

Rakaia

Christchurch

Canterbury Plains

Banks Peninsula

Ashburton

Timaru

PACIFIC OCEAN

Oamaru

Wool New Zealand ranks second only to Australia among the world's top wool producers. It has about 50 million sheep, about half of which live on South Island.

Royal albatross This impressive bird, which can have a wingspan of more than 10 feet (3 meters), spends most of its time at sea. It comes ashore only to breed on a few islands near New Zealand and the southern tip of South America.

Trekking or tramping (hiking) is a way of enjoying the mountain scenery of South Island. Many trekkers believe that the 54-km (34-mile) Milford Track over Mackinnon Pass is the most beautiful walk in the world. Tourism is growing in importance in New Zealand.

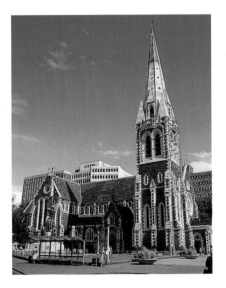

Christchurch, the largest city on South Island, lies on the edge of the Canterbury Plains, one of New Zealand's leading wheat-growing and sheep-raising regions. Many of the city's industries process farm products. Christchurch was founded in 1851.

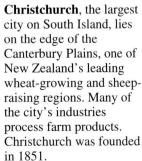

PACIFIC OCEAN

The Pacific is the largest and deepest of the world's four oceans. It covers about one-third of the world's surface. It stretches from the Bering Strait, which links it to the icy Arctic Ocean in the north, to Antarctica in the south. The Pacific is widest near the equator. Between mainland Malaysia and Panama, it is about 24,000 km (15,000 miles) wide.

The Pacific contains many islands. Some of the islands are high and mountainous, others low and flat. The mountainous islands are active or dormant volcanoes that rise from the ocean floor. Other islands are low-lying, rising only a few meters above sea level. These are made of coral. The Pacific islands are divided into three geographical and cultural groups: Melanesia, Micronesia, and Polynesia.

PACIFIC OCEAN
Area: 181,000,000 sq km (69,884,500 sq miles)
Average depth: 3,940 m (12,900 ft)
Deepest point: Mariana Trench 11,033 m (36,198 ft)

International Date Line
This imaginary line roughly corresponds to the 180° line of longitude that runs through the Pacific. Because time is measured east and west of Greenwich, England, (0°) at a rate of one hour per 15 degrees, there is a difference of 24 hours at the 180° line of longitude. Travellers from west to east gain a day as they cross the line, those going east-west lose one.

Whales can be seen off many Pacific coasts. These great mammals divide their time between warm seas, where they give birth, and cold seas, where feeding is good. The blue whale, which is the largest animal that has ever lived, is found in all oceans, but whaling has made it scarce.

ASIA

NORTH

Bering Strait

Midway (US)

Hawaii (US)

Johnston (US)

International Date Line

Northern Mariana Is (US)

MARSHALL ISLANDS

Guam (US)

MICRONESIA

FEDERATED STATES OF MICRONESIA

PALAU

NAURU

KIRIBATI

PAPUA NEW GUINEA

SOLOMON ISLANDS

TUVALU

Wallis & Futuna (Fr)

SAMOA

American Samoa

Cook Is (NZ)

MELANESIA

VANUATU

New Caledonia (Fr)

FIJI

TONGA

P O L

AUSTRALIA

Norfolk (Aus)

Kermadec Is (NZ)

NEW ZEALAND

SOUTH

Chatham Is (NZ)

Bounty Is (NZ)

Auckland Is (NZ)

Macquarie Is (Aus)

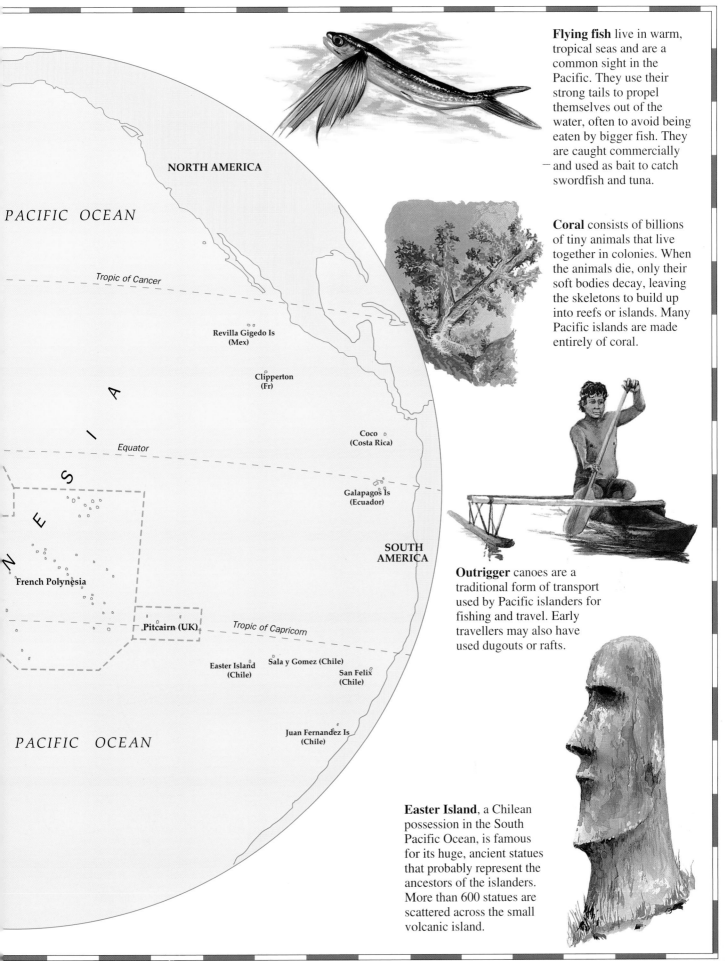

Flying fish live in warm, tropical seas and are a common sight in the Pacific. They use their strong tails to propel themselves out of the water, often to avoid being eaten by bigger fish. They are caught commercially and used as bait to catch swordfish and tuna.

Coral consists of billions of tiny animals that live together in colonies. When the animals die, only their soft bodies decay, leaving the skeletons to build up into reefs or islands. Many Pacific islands are made entirely of coral.

Outrigger canoes are a traditional form of transport used by Pacific islanders for fishing and travel. Early travellers may also have used dugouts or rafts.

Easter Island, a Chilean possession in the South Pacific Ocean, is famous for its huge, ancient statues that probably represent the ancestors of the islanders. More than 600 statues are scattered across the small volcanic island.

NORTH AMERICA

PACIFIC OCEAN

Tropic of Cancer

Revilla Gigedo Is
(Mex)

Clipperton
(Fr)

Coco
(Costa Rica)

Equator

Galapagos Is
(Ecuador)

SOUTH
AMERICA

French Polynesia

Pitcairn (UK)

Tropic of Capricorn

Easter Island
(Chile)

Sala y Gomez (Chile)

San Felix
(Chile)

Juan Fernandez Is
(Chile)

PACIFIC OCEAN

MELANESIA

Melanesia includes four independent countries and two territories. Papua New Guinea is by far the largest country in the region. It consists of numerous islands and the eastern part of the island of New Guinea. The western part belongs to Indonesia. The other three independent countries of Melanesia are, in order of size, Solomon Islands, Fiji, and Vanuatu. Vanuatu was formerly ruled jointly by Britain and France and called New Hebrides.

Volcanoes are common on the islands of Papua New Guinea, and many are active. These volcanoes form part of an unstable part of the earth called the Pacific ''ring of fire.''

PAPUA NEW GUINEA

• Madang

New Britain

▲ Mount Wilhelm 14,880 feet (4,509 m) • Lae

Gulf of Papua

Port Moresby

PAPUA NEW GUINEA

Area: 462,840 sq km (178,704 sq miles)
Highest point: Mt Wilhelm 4,509 m (14,793 ft)
Population: 4,501,000
Capital and largest city: Port Moresby (pop 193,000)
Official language: English
Religions: Christianity (Protestant 56%, Roman Catholic 32%), traditional beliefs
Government: Constitutional monarchy
Currency: Kina

FIJI

Area: 18,274 sq km (7,056 sq miles)
Highest point: Mt Tomanivi, on Viti Levu, 1,323 m (4,341 ft)
Population: 815,000
Capital and largest city: Suva (pop 167,000)
Official language: English
Religions: Christianity (53%), Hinduism (38%), Islam (8%)
Government: Republic
Currency: Fiji dollar

SOLOMON ISLANDS

Area: 28,896 sq km (11,157 sq miles)
Highest point: Mt Makarakomburu 2,447 m (8,028 ft)
Population: 403,000
Capital and largest city: Honiara (pop 44,000)
Official language: English
Religions: Christianity (97%)
Government: Constitutional monarchy
Currency: Solomon Islands dollar

VANUATU

Area: 12,189 sq km (4,706 sq miles)
Highest point: Mt Tabwemasana 1,879 m (6,165 ft)
Population: 177,000
Capital and largest city: Port-Vila (pop 19,000)
Official languages: Bislama, English, French
Religions: Christianity (72%)
Government: Republic
Currency: Vatu

Territories
New Caledonia (French overseas territory)
Norfolk Island (Australian territory)

Tourism is important in Fiji and elsewhere in Melanesia because it provides jobs for local people. Many remote Pacific islands hold out hope for the development of the tourist industry.

Mining is important in Papua New Guinea, which exports oil, copper, gold, and other metals. One island, Bougainville, has a huge copper mine. The people there objected to the mining and fought a long civil war, which began in the late 1980s and continued until a peace agreement was signed in 1998.

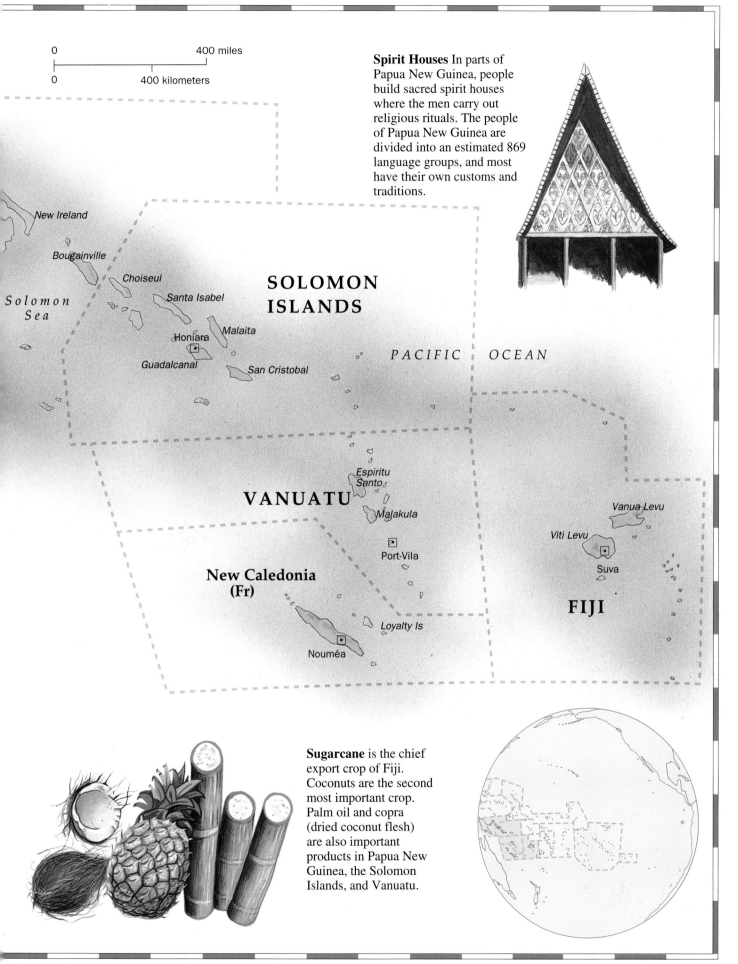

Spirit Houses In parts of Papua New Guinea, people build sacred spirit houses where the men carry out religious rituals. The people of Papua New Guinea are divided into an estimated 869 language groups, and most have their own customs and traditions.

0   400 miles

0   400 kilometers

New Ireland

Bougainville

Choiseul

Solomon Sea

Santa Isabel

SOLOMON ISLANDS

Honiara

Malaita

Guadalcanal

San Cristobal

PACIFIC OCEAN

Espiritu Santo

VANUATU

Malakula

Port-Vila

New Caledonia (Fr)

Loyalty Is

Nouméa

Vanua Levu

Viti Levu

Suva

FIJI

Sugarcane is the chief export crop of Fiji. Coconuts are the second most important crop. Palm oil and copra (dried coconut flesh) are also important products in Papua New Guinea, the Solomon Islands, and Vanuatu.

MICRONESIA

Micronesia includes the Pacific islands north of Melanesia, which number more than 2,000. Most of them are small, low-lying coral islands.

The largest country in Micronesia is the Republic of Kiribati (formerly the Gilbert Islands). It became independent in 1979. The Federated States of Micronesia and the Republic of the Marshall Islands are former US territories. They became independent in 1991. The Republic of Palau, which became independent in 1994, is another former US territory. The tiny Republic of Nauru became independent in 1968.

Sharks are common in the warm waters of the central Pacific. All sharks are carnivores, but most of the 350 species are small and timid. Only a few eat large fishes, and very few are big enough to attack people.

KIRIBATI

Area: 726 sq km (280 sq miles)
Highest point: 81 m (266 ft) on Banaba Island
Population: 83,000
Capital and largest city: Bairiki on Tarawa Atoll (pop 25,000)
Official language: English
Religions: Christianity
Government: Republic
Currency: Australian dollar

REPUBLIC OF THE MARSHALL ISLANDS

Area: 181 sq km (70 sq miles)
Highest point: 10 m (33 ft) on Likiep
Population: 60,000
Capital and largest city: Dalap-Uliga-Darrit on Majuro (pop 28,000)
Official language: English
Religions: Christianity
Government: Republic
Currency: US dollar

FEDERATED STATES OF MICRONESIA

Area: 702 sq km (271 sq miles)
Highest point: Totolom 791 m (2,595 ft)
Population: 111,000
Capital: Palikir on Pohnpei
Official language: English
Religions: Christianity
Government: Federal republic
Currency: US dollar

PALAU

Area: 459 sq km (177 sq miles)
Highest point: Mt Ngerchelchauus 242m (794 ft)
Population: 17,000
Capital and largest city: Koror (pop 12,000)
Official languages: Palauan, English
Religions: Christianity
Government: Republic
Currency: US dollar

NAURU

Area: 21 sq km (8 sq miles)
Highest point: 61 m (200 ft)
Population: 10,000
Capital: none
Official language: Nauruan
Religions: Christianity
Government: Republic
Currency: Australian dollar

Territories
Guam (US territory)
Northern Mariana Islands (US commonwealth)
Wake Island (US possession)

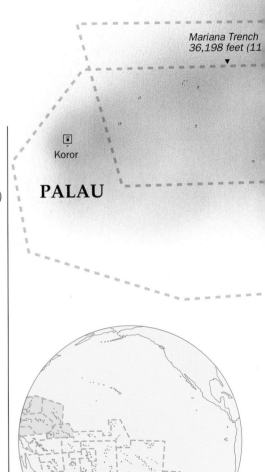

Mariana Trench 36,198 feet (11

Koror

PALAU

Palau Islands This nation group of mostly tiny islands is surrounded by a coral reef. Some are covered by thick forests, and the people grow coconuts and fruit crops. Others are rugged and uninhabited.

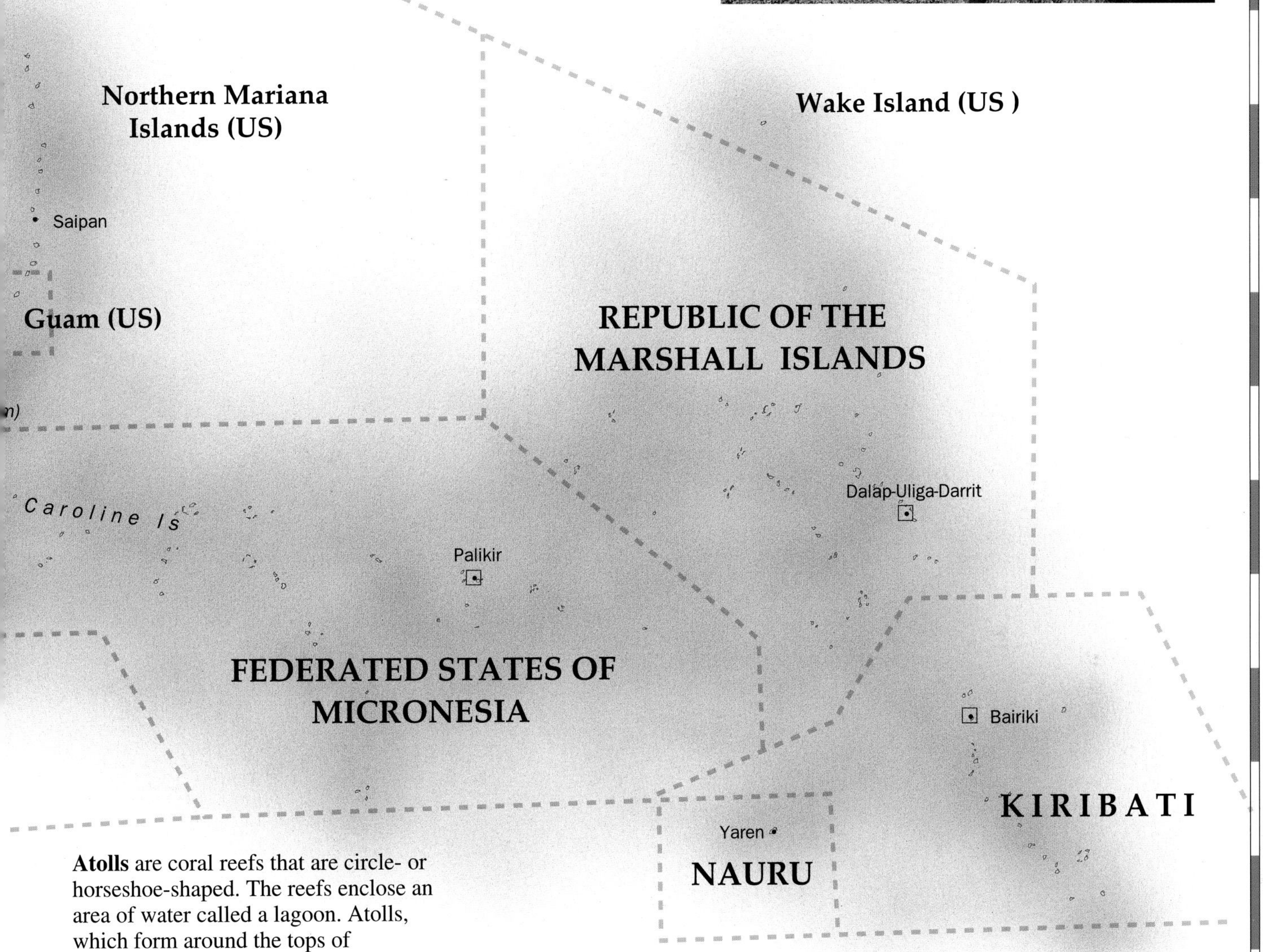

0 |————————————————| 400 miles

0 |————————————————| 400 kilometers

Northern Mariana Islands (US)

• Saipan

Guam (US)

n)

Caroline Is

Wake Island (US)

REPUBLIC OF THE MARSHALL ISLANDS

Dalap-Uliga-Darrit
⊡

Palikir
⊡

FEDERATED STATES OF MICRONESIA

⊡ Bairiki

KIRIBATI

Yaren •

NAURU

Atolls are coral reefs that are circle- or horseshoe-shaped. The reefs enclose an area of water called a lagoon. Atolls, which form around the tops of submerged volcanoes, are common throughout Micronesia.

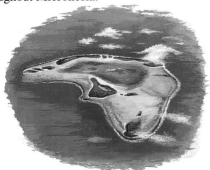

Phosphate rock is used to make fertilizers. The central plateau of Nauru has deposits of high-grade phosphate rock, and the mining of the rock has brought prosperity to the island. The deposits are, however, likely to be exhausted by 2008.

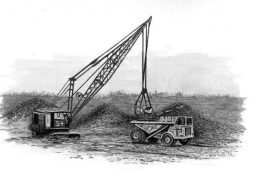

POLYNESIA

Polynesia covers a vast area in the Pacific Ocean, between Midway Island in the north, New Zealand in the southwest, and Easter Island in the southeast.

   This vast expanse of water contains three independent countries and several territories, listed below. The largest country is Samoa, which was formerly called Western Samoa. Samoa was once ruled by New Zealand, but it became fully independent in 1962. Tonga, which consists of more than 170 islands, was a British protectorate, but it became independent in 1970. Tuvalu, formerly the British Ellice Islands, became independent in 1978.

Sea turtles live throughout the Pacific Ocean. Females spend their lives in the sea, returning to the land only to lay their eggs. Most males never return to land after they enter the sea as hatchlings. Most species are endangered.

SAMOA

Area: 2,813 sq km (1,086 sq miles)
Highest point: Mauga Silisli 1,858 m (6,096 ft)
Population: 174,000
Capital and largest city: Apia (pop 34,000)
Official languages: Samoan, English
Religions: Christianity
Government: Constitutional monarchy
Currency: Tala

TONGA

Area: 747 sq km (288 sq miles)
Highest point: Mt Kao 1,033 m (3,389 ft)
Population: 98,000
Capital and largest city: Nuku'alofa (pop 21,000)
Official languages: Tongan, English
Religions: Christianity
Government: Constitutional monarchy
Currency: Pa'anga

TUVALU

Area: 26 sq km (10 sq miles)
Highest point: 4.6 m (15 ft) on Niulakita
Population: 10,500
Capital and largest city: Fongafale on Funafuti island (pop 4,000)
Official language: none
Religions: Christianity
Government: Constitutional monarchy
Currency: Tuvalu dollar

Shells As well as eating the contents of some of them, Pacific islanders use shells to make jewelry and ornaments for the tourist trade. Once shells were used as money, and today collectors still pay high prices for the rarest deep water shells.

Territories

American Samoa (US territory)
Cook Islands (self-governing territory in association with New Zealand)
Easter Island (Chilean dependency)
French Polynesia (French overseas territory)
Midway Island (US possession)
Niue (New Zealand)
Pitcairn Islands Group (British overseas territory)
Tokelau (New Zealand territory)
Wallis & Futuna Islands (French overseas territory)

Hawaii (US State)

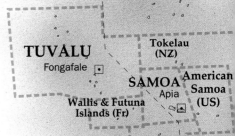

Midway Island (US)

Johnston Island (US)

Phoenix Is

TUVALU
Fongafale

Tokelau (NZ)

SAMOA
Apia

American Samoa (US)

Wallis & Futuna Islands (Fr)

TONGA
Nuku'alofa

Niue (NZ)

International Date Line

NEW ZEALAND

Flowers grow in huge numbers profusion in the tropics, and islanders wear them as decoration. Garlands of flowers are a traditional gift of welcome for visitors to many Polynesian islands. The Polynesians are renowned for their hospitality and kindness to visitors.

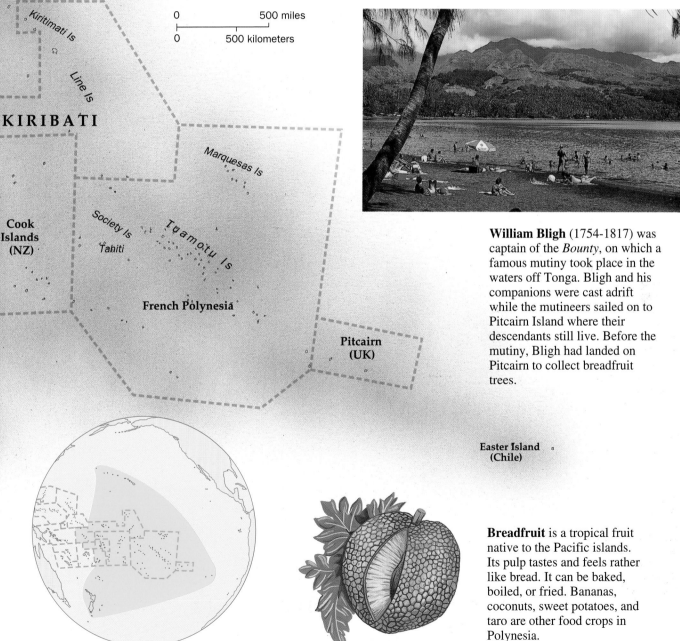

Hawaii
(US)

Kiritimati Is

Line Is

KIRIBATI

Marquesas Is

Cook
Islands
(NZ)

Society Is

Tahiti

Tuamotu Is

French Polynesia

Pitcairn
(UK)

Easter Island
(Chile)

0   500 miles

0   500 kilometers

William Bligh (1754-1817) was captain of the *Bounty*, on which a famous mutiny took place in the waters off Tonga. Bligh and his companions were cast adrift while the mutineers sailed on to Pitcairn Island where their descendants still live. Before the mutiny, Bligh had landed on Pitcairn to collect breadfruit trees.

Breadfruit is a tropical fruit native to the Pacific islands. Its pulp tastes and feels rather like bread. It can be baked, boiled, or fried. Bananas, coconuts, sweet potatoes, and taro are other food crops in Polynesia.

PEOPLE AND BELIEFS

Australia, New Zealand, and the Pacific islands cover a vast area, but they contain less than 1 percent of the world's population. Much of the region, including most of the interior of Australia, is thinly populated or empty of people. Most Australians live along the eastern, southeastern, and southwestern coasts in large cities, notably Sydney, Melbourne, Brisbane, Adelaide, and Perth. Much of Papua New Guinea is covered by thinly populated rainforests. New Zealand, with its fertile farmland and its many cities and towns, is the most densely populated of the three main countries in the region.

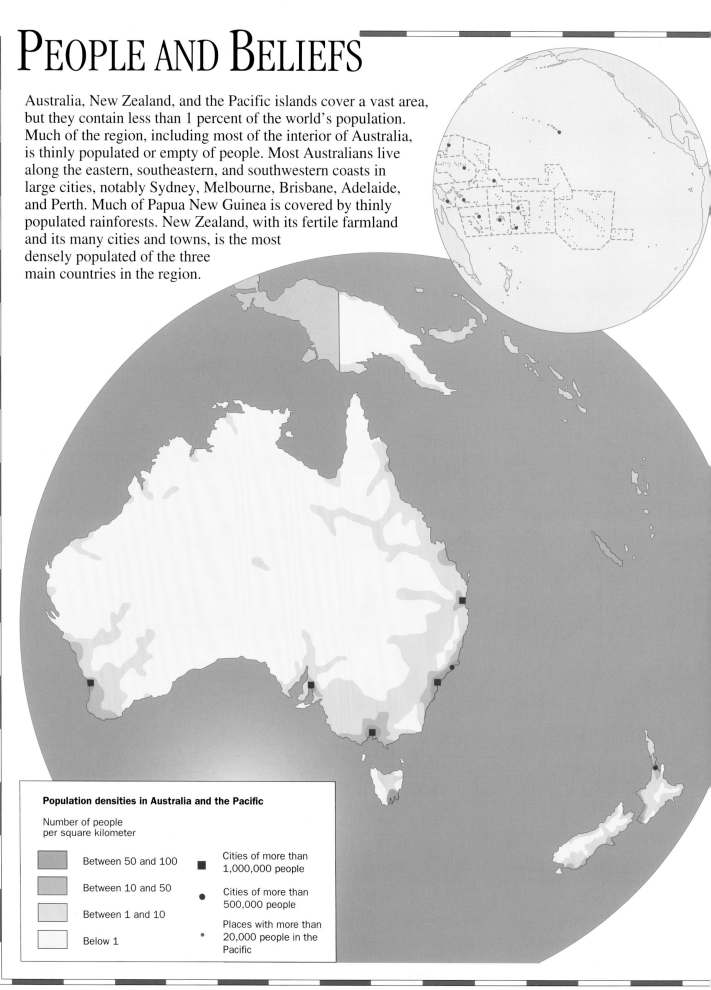

Population densities in Australia and the Pacific

Number of people
per square kilometer

Between 50 and 100

Between 10 and 50

Between 1 and 10

Below 1

■ Cities of more than 1,000,000 people

● Cities of more than 500,000 people

• Places with more than 20,000 people in the Pacific

Population and Area

Australia, the smallest of the world's seven continents, covers 91 percent of the land in the Pacific region. It also contains more than 60 percent of the total population. Papua New Guinea and New Zealand rank second and third in both area and population. Some of the small Pacific island nations, including Fiji, Samoa, Tonga, and Tuvalu, are much more densely populated than the three largest countries.

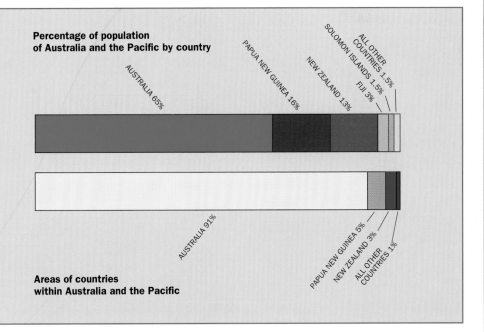

Percentage of population of Australia and the Pacific by country

AUSTRALIA 65% | PAPUA NEW GUINEA 16% | NEW ZEALAND 13% | FIJI 3% | SOLOMON ISLANDS 1.5% | ALL OTHER COUNTRIES 1.5%

AUSTRALIA 91% | PAPUA NEW GUINEA 5% | NEW ZEALAND 3% | ALL OTHER COUNTRIES 1%

Areas of countries within Australia and the Pacific

Main Religions

Before the arrival of European missionaries in the late 18th century, most people in Australia and the Pacific followed ancient religions based on a belief in spirits and numerous gods. The people told many stories about how the gods created the world and how they still interact with people during religious ceremonies.

For example, the aboriginal people of Australia believed that the world was created by gods and goddesses during a period called the Dreaming. The spirits of these gods had merged with nature and could be contacted through rituals.

Christian missionaries worked hard to stamp out traditional beliefs.

Today, most of the people are Christians. The religious beliefs of the people reflect their countries of origin. For example, people of Irish, French, or Italian ancestry are usually members of the Roman Catholic Church, while people of English origin are often Anglicans. Immigrants from Asia are usually Muslims, Hindus, or Buddhists.

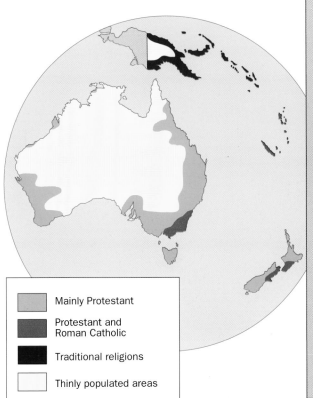

Mainly Protestant

Protestant and Roman Catholic

Traditional religions

Thinly populated areas

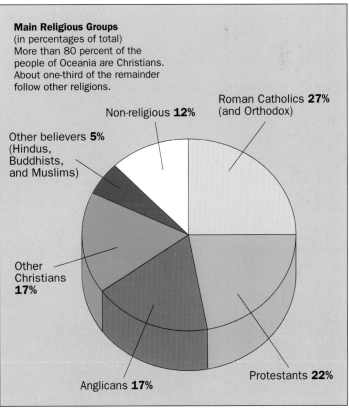

Main Religious Groups
(in percentages of total)
More than 80 percent of the people of Oceania are Christians. About one-third of the remainder follow other religions.

Non-religious **12%**

Roman Catholics **27%** (and Orthodox)

Other believers **5%** (Hindus, Buddhists, and Muslims)

Other Christians **17%**

Anglicans **17%**

Protestants **22%**

CLIMATE AND VEGETATION

Papua New Guinea, the Solomon Islands, Vanuatu, and many other Pacific islands lie in the tropics. This region has a hot climate, often with heavy rainfall, and rainforests cover much of the land. The northern part of Australia also lies in the tropics. It has a hot, wet summer season (between November and April) and a hot, dry winter season (May to October). The interior of Australia is dry, containing deserts and dry grasslands. Southern Australia has four seasons, with most of the rain falling in winter. New Zealand has a mild, rainy climate, although the mountains in South Island have cold, snowy winters. North Island has a warmer climate than South Island.

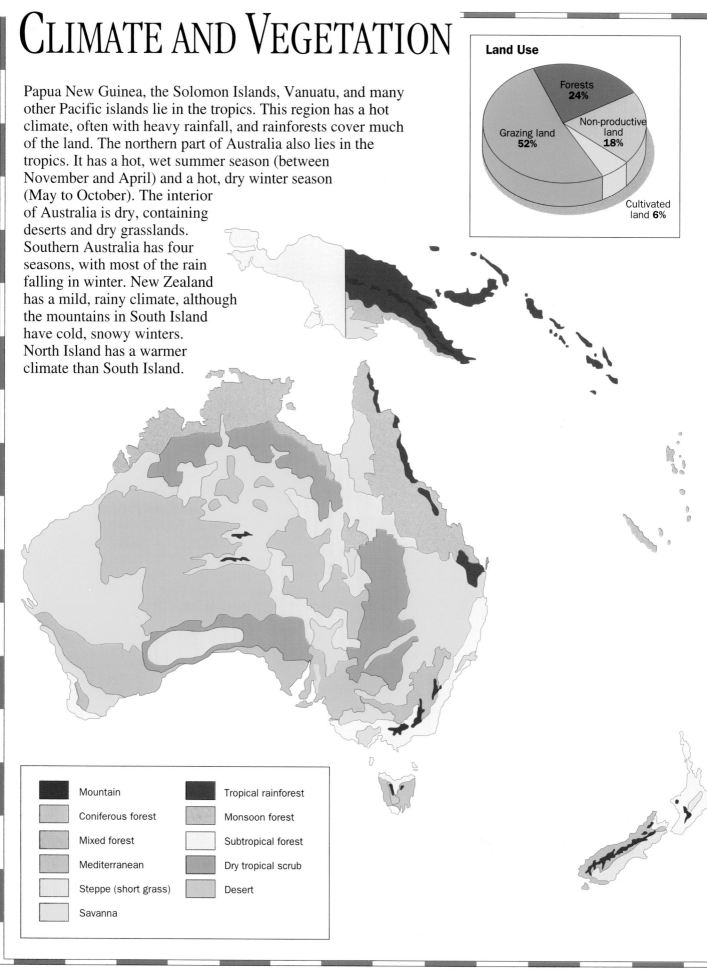

Land Use

- Forests 24%
- Grazing land 52%
- Non-productive land 18%
- Cultivated land 6%

Mountain	Tropical rainforest
Coniferous forest	Monsoon forest
Mixed forest	Subtropical forest
Mediterranean	Dry tropical scrub
Steppe (short grass)	Desert
Savanna	

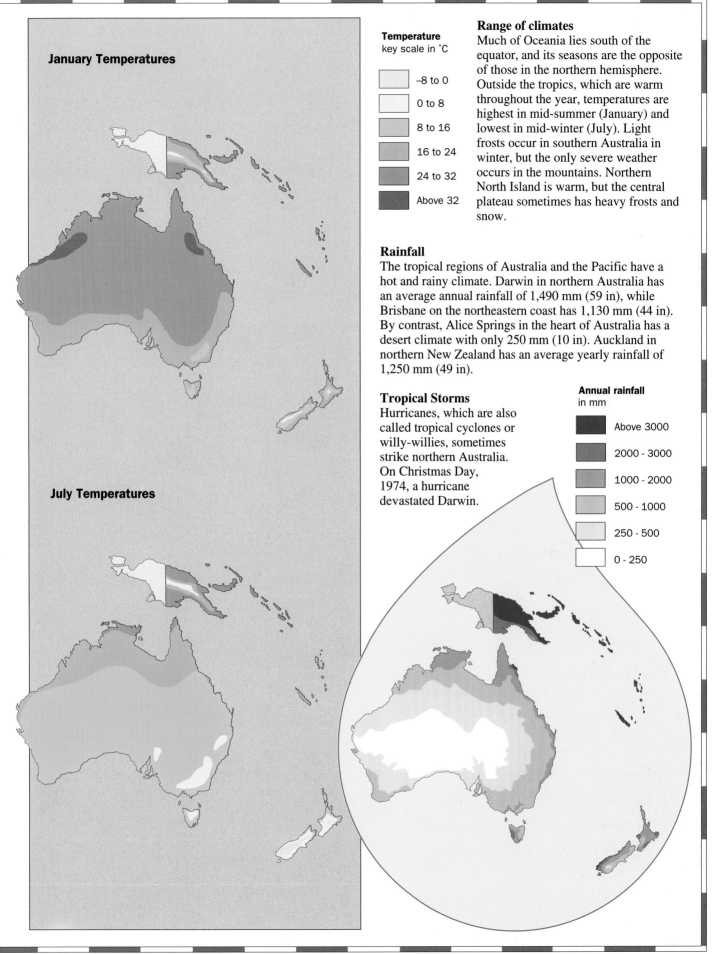

January Temperatures

July Temperatures

Temperature
key scale in ˚C

	–8 to 0
	0 to 8
	8 to 16
	16 to 24
	24 to 32
	Above 32

Range of climates

Much of Oceania lies south of the equator, and its seasons are the opposite of those in the northern hemisphere. Outside the tropics, which are warm throughout the year, temperatures are highest in mid-summer (January) and lowest in mid-winter (July). Light frosts occur in southern Australia in winter, but the only severe weather occurs in the mountains. Northern North Island is warm, but the central plateau sometimes has heavy frosts and snow.

Rainfall

The tropical regions of Australia and the Pacific have a hot and rainy climate. Darwin in northern Australia has an average annual rainfall of 1,490 mm (59 in), while Brisbane on the northeastern coast has 1,130 mm (44 in). By contrast, Alice Springs in the heart of Australia has a desert climate with only 250 mm (10 in). Auckland in northern New Zealand has an average yearly rainfall of 1,250 mm (49 in).

Tropical Storms

Hurricanes, which are also called tropical cyclones or willy-willies, sometimes strike northern Australia. On Christmas Day, 1974, a hurricane devastated Darwin.

Annual rainfall
in mm

	Above 3000
	2000 - 3000
	1000 - 2000
	500 - 1000
	250 - 500
	0 - 250

ECOLOGY AND ENVIRONMENT

Around 200 million years ago, all of the world's continents were grouped together. But about 180 million years ago, this single, huge landmass began to break up, and Australia became isolated from the other land areas. As a result, its plants and animals evolved differently from those of other landmasses. None of its mammals give birth to fully formed babies, like those in the rest of the world. The aboriginal peoples modified the land through hunting and farming, but their effect was small compared with that of the Europeans. European settlement during the last two centuries badly damaged the fragile environments of Australia, New Zealand, and other Pacific islands.

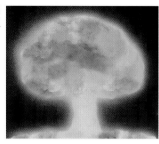

After vigorous protests by pressure groups and governments, nuclear testing in the Pacific has stopped, but nobody knows how much long-term environmental damage it caused to the region.

Environmental Damage to Land and Sea

- Existing desert
- Area at risk of desertification
- Present rainforest
- Rainforest seriously damaged in recent years
- Most polluted seas
- Most polluted rivers
- ☢ Former nuclear test sites
- Coastline at risk by global warming
- Island groups at risk by global warming

Vanishing Islands

Because of air pollution, the world is becoming warmer. Global warming may be melting the ice that covers of Antarctica and other areas. Melting of ice sheets will raise sea levels and threaten low-lying islands in the Pacific. For example, two small islands in Kiribati have already disappeared, and the Marshall Islands, Tokelau, and Tuvalu, as well as coastal areas in Australia, are threatened by the rising sea.

Damaging the Environment

European farming methods have damaged the land. In dry areas, huge herds of cattle and sheep have stripped away the dry grasses and turned the land into desert. Forest clearance has led to a loss of three-quarters of Australia's tropical forest, while more than one-third of the country's woodland has been cut down or severely damaged. This destruction has led to the extinctions of many animal species.

Settlers rashly introduced plants and animals from Europe. After rabbits were released into the wild, they stripped the land bare and helped turn grasslands into deserts. Other new animals, including foxes and domestic cats, preyed on indigenous animals and helped make them extinct.

One famous natural wonder, the Great Barrier Reef, is now threatened by pollution and by damage caused by tourists.

Radioactive contamination has also occurred in Australia and on some Pacific islands where nuclear weapons have been tested. Today many people are aware of the threat to the environment and are working to conserve the region's wildlife.

Natural Hazards

Earthquakes and volcanoes occur in a zone running from Papua New Guinea, through the Solomon Islands to Vanuatu. Another zone stretches from Samoa to New Zealand. These zones are part of the Pacific "ring of fire." Other natural hazards include storms, droughts and bush fires.

The Great Barrier Reef, one of the world's richest ecosystems, is periodically threatened by the crown-of-thorns starfish, which attacks the coral. Scientists are still trying to find out why sudden explosions of the starfish population occur.

Natural Hazards

- Earthquake zones
- ▲ Active volcanoes
- Areas affected by annual tropical cyclones (January - March)
- Recent droughts
- Areas recently hit by major bush fires

Endangered Species

Australia has a higher rate of extinction of mammals than any other continent in the world. One famous example is the Tasmanian wolf, which was hunted to extinction by farmers wanting to protect their livestock. In New Zealand, the moa, a flightless bird, was also hunted to extinction by Polynesian peoples. Many extinctions have occurred on the Pacific islands.

Today, conservation is an important issue. In Australia, the National Parks and Wildlife Service is seeking to halt the rate of extinctions that have marked the last 200 years, while New Zealand now protects most of its native species. In both countries, thousands of people have joined demonstrations against developments that may harm the environment.

Some endangered species

Birds
Akiapolaau (Hawaiian finch)
Australian ground parrot
Black stilt (New Zealand)
Kagu (New Caledonia)
Kakapo (New Zealand)
Short-tailed albatross (Pacific)

Mammals and Reptiles
Brush-tailed rat kangaroo (Aus)
Leadbeater's possum (Aus)
Northern hairy-nosed wombat (Aus)
Numbat (Aus)
Tuatara (New Zealand)

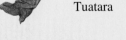
Tuatara

Trees and plants
Kauri tree (New Zealand)

Economy

Australia and New Zealand are prosperous countries, but most of the Pacific islands are far less developed. Until about 50 years ago, the economy of the region was based on farming. Australia and New Zealand were major producers of dairy products, especially butter and cheese, lamb, sugar, wheat, and wool. Enormous quantities of these goods were sold to the industrial countries of Europe.

Australia is also a major world producer of minerals. Today its mines yield minerals such as bauxite, coal, copper, diamonds, manganese, nickel, oil and natural gas, silver, tin, tungsten, and zinc, which it exports to industrial countries in Asia, including Japan. But manufacturing is now the most important economic activity in both Australia and New Zealand.

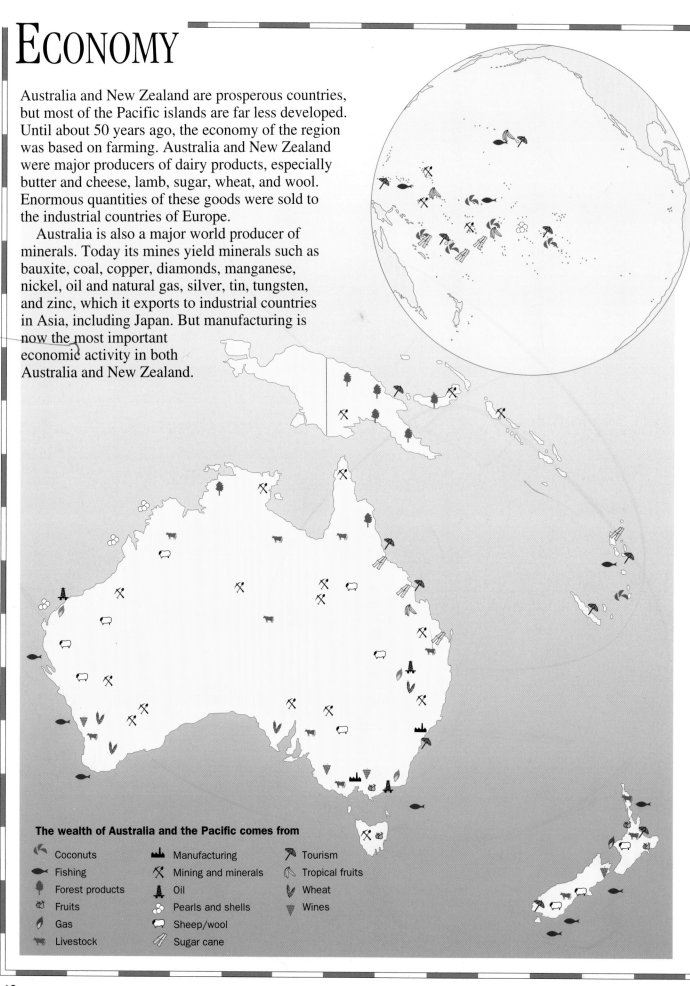

The wealth of Australia and the Pacific comes from

🌴	Coconuts	🏭	Manufacturing	☂	Tourism
🐟	Fishing	⚒	Mining and minerals	🍌	Tropical fruits
🌲	Forest products	🛢	Oil	🌾	Wheat
🍎	Fruits	🦪	Pearls and shells	🍇	Wines
🍃	Gas	🐑	Sheep/wool		
🐄	Livestock	⚒	Sugar cane		

42

Gross National Product

To compare the economies of countries, experts calculate the gross national product (GNP) of the countries in US dollars. The GNP is the total value of the goods and services produced by a country in a year. The chart shows that the country with the highest GNP is Australia. Its total GNP in 1997 was about one-twentieth that of the United States. Following Australia come New Zealand, Papua New Guinea, and Fiji.

GNP for the countries of Australia and the Pacific (in billions of dollars)

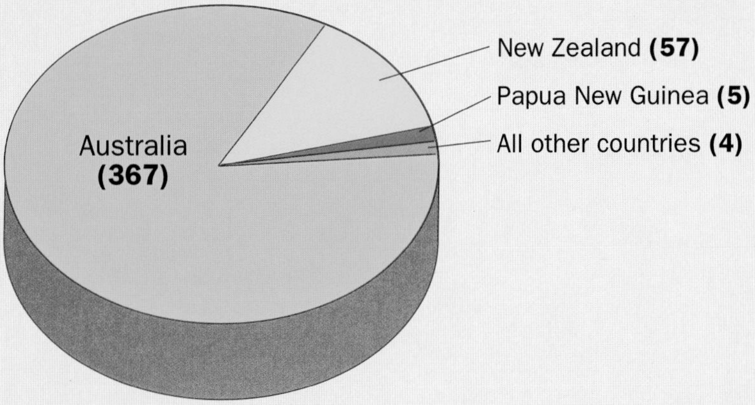

Australia (367)
New Zealand (57)
Papua New Guinea (5)
All other countries (4)

Sources of Energy

Australia has abundant energy-producing resources. Coal is the major source of energy. The main coalfields are in Queensland and New South Wales. Australia also exports coal. Victoria and Western Australia also produce oil and natural gas. Hydroelectric plants, especially those in the Snowy Mountains and in Tasmania, produce about 11 percent of Australia's energy supply.

Hydroelectric plants, especially on the Waikato River on North Island and on the Clutha and Waitaki rivers on South Island, account for much of the electrical energy produced in New Zealand. Thermal energy is also obtained from volcanic steam on North Island. New Zealand also produces coal.

Per Capita GNPs

Per capita means per head or per person. Per capita GNPs are worked out by dividing the GNP by the population. For example, the per capita GNP of Australia is US $20,650. By contrast, the Solomon Islands has a per capita GNP of only $870, which places it among the world's poorer countries.

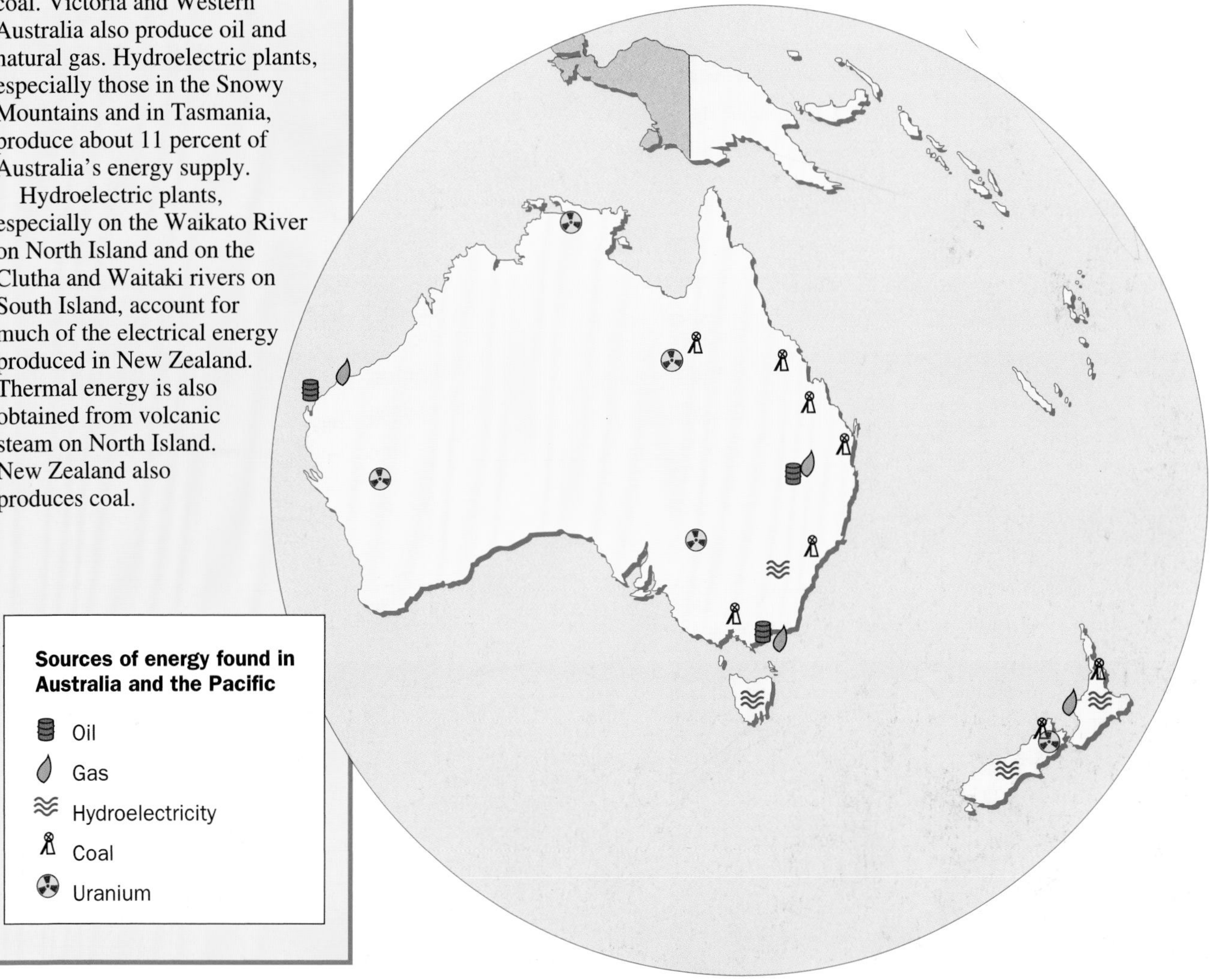

Sources of energy found in Australia and the Pacific

- 🛢 Oil
- 💧 Gas
- ≈ Hydroelectricity
- ♨ Coal
- ☢ Uranium

POLITICS AND HISTORY

Britain played a major part in the modern history of Australia and New Zealand. But after Britain joined the European Economic Community (now the European Union) in 1973, the ties with Britain were loosened, though both countries remain members of the Commonwealth and cultural relationships are strong. Since 1973, Australia and New Zealand have found new markets for their exports, with trading partners in eastern Asia and North America.

Another political issue is the status of the first people in the region, including the aboriginal and Torres Strait Islander people of Australia and the Maori of New Zealand. In the 1990s, conflict occurred in Fiji between the native Fijians and the descendants of Indians who came to Fiji to work on sugar plantations.

Great events
The original inhabitants of Australia and the Pacific islands came from southeastern Asia thousands of years ago. European settlement on a large scale began only in the 19th century. The first settlers were convicts who worked in penal colonies, but they were soon followed by free settlers. The settlers took over aboriginal lands and brought diseases that killed the people because they had no natural immunity. Within 200 years the Aborigines were outnumbered by more than 50 to one. The British introduced sheep and cattle to their new colonies, discovered gold, and developed industries and commerce. In the late 19th century Britain, France, Germany, and the United States competed for control of the islands of the Pacific. However, since the 1960s, some 12 Pacific countries have won their independence. Today Australia and New Zealand are prosperous independent countries that trade all round the world, and especially with the United States and Japan.

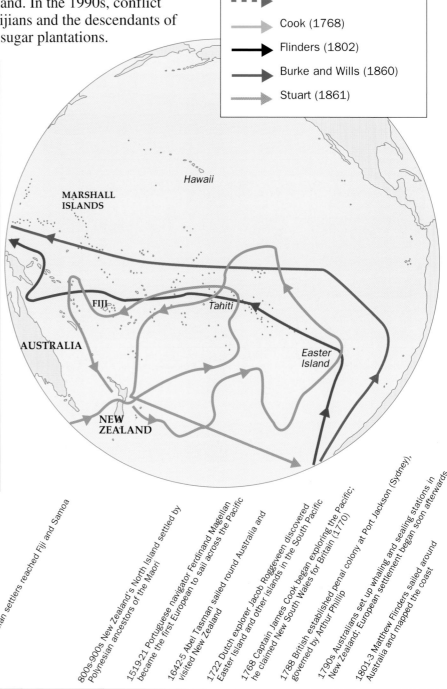

Exploring Australia and the Pacific

Pacific
- ➤ Magellan (1519)
- ➤ Roggeveen (1721)
- ➤ Cook (1772)

Australia
- ➤ Tasman (1642 & 1644)
- ┈┈➤
- ➤ Cook (1768)
- ➤ Flinders (1802)
- ➤ Burke and Wills (1860)
- ➤ Stuart (1861)

Map labels: Hawaii, MARSHALL ISLANDS, FIJI, Tahiti, AUSTRALIA, Easter Island, NEW ZEALAND

Important dates

- **40,000** Humans already settled in Australia
- **7000s** Cultivators settled in New Guinea
- **5000s** Sea levels rose and isolated Australia, New Zealand, and Papua New Guinea
- **3000** Aboriginal rock paintings
- **1300s** Melanesian settlers reached Fiji and Samoa
- **800s–900s** New Zealand's North Island settled by Polynesian ancestors of the Maori
- **1519–21** Portuguese navigator Ferdinand Magellan became the first European to sail across the Pacific
- **1642–5** Abel Tasman sailed round Australia and visited New Zealand
- **1722** Dutch explorer Jacob Roggeveen discovered Easter Island and other islands in the South Pacific
- **1768** Captain James Cook began exploring the Pacific; he claimed New South Wales for Britain (1770)
- **1788** British established penal colony at Port Jackson (Sydney), governed by Arthur Phillip
- **1790s** Australians set up whaling and sealing stations in New Zealand; European settlement began soon afterwards
- **1801–3** Matthew Flinders sailed around Australia and mapped the coast

40,000BC	AD1

44

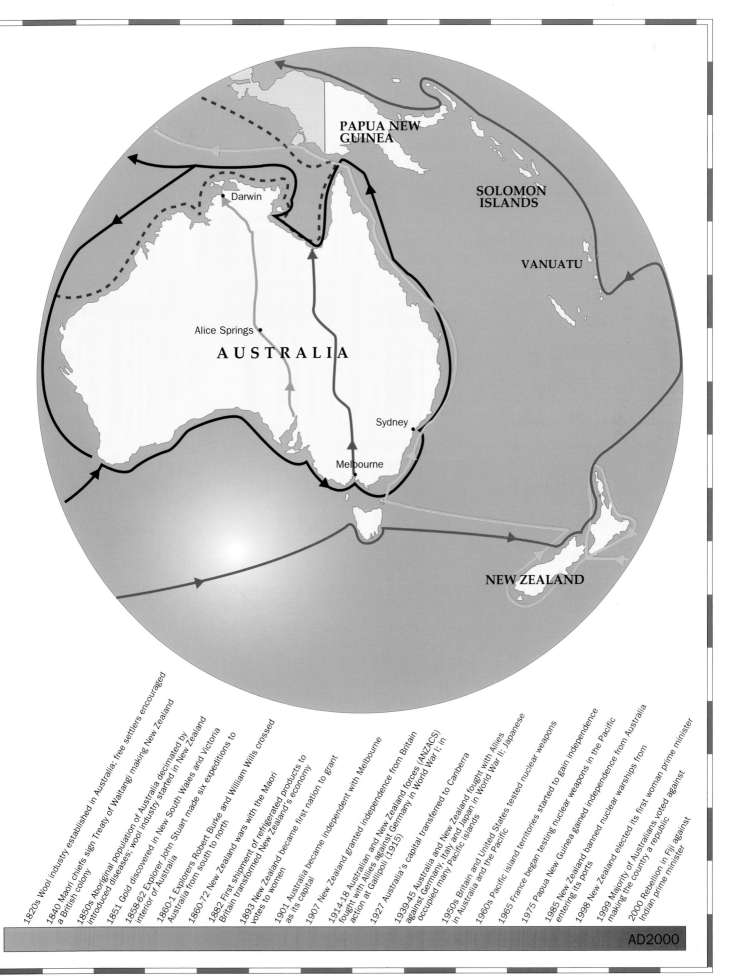

PAPUA NEW GUINEA

SOLOMON ISLANDS

VANUATU

Darwin

Alice Springs •

A U S T R A L I A

Sydney •

Melbourne •

NEW ZEALAND

1820s Wool industry established in Australia; free settlers encouraged

1840 Maori chiefs sign Treaty of Waitangi making New Zealand a British colony

1850s Aboriginal population of Australia decimated by introduced diseases; wool industry started in New Zealand

1851 Gold discovered in New South Wales and Victoria

1858-62 Explorer John Stuart made six expeditions to interior of Australia

1860-1 Explorers Robert Burke and William Wills crossed Australia from south to north

1860-72 New Zealand wars with the Maori

1882 First shipment of refrigerated products to Britain transformed New Zealand's economy

1893 New Zealand became first nation to grant votes to women

1901 Australia became independent with Melbourne as its capital

1907 New Zealand granted independence from Britain

1914-18 Australian and New Zealand forces (ANZACS) fought with Allies against Germany in World War I; in action at Gallipoli (1915)

1927 Australia's capital transferred to Canberra

1939-45 Australia and New Zealand fought with Allies against Germany, Italy and Japan in World War II; Japanese occupied many Pacific Islands

1950s Britain and United States tested nuclear weapons in Australia and the Pacific

1960s Pacific island territories started to gain independence

1965 France began testing nuclear weapons in the Pacific

1975 Papua New Guinea gained independence from Australia

1985 New Zealand banned nuclear warships from entering its ports

1998 New Zealand elected its first woman prime minister

1999 Majority of Australians voted against making the country a republic

2000 Rebellion in Fiji against Indian prime minister

AD2000

45

INDEX

Numbers in **bold** are map references
Numbers in *italics* are picture references